Minding My Own Business

Creating A Business That Works

By

Dirk T. Dieters

authorHOUSE

1663 Liberty Drive, Suite 200
Bloomington, Indiana 47403
(800) 839-8640
www.AuthorHouse.com

This book is a work of non-fiction. Unless otherwise noted, the author and the publisher make no explicit guarantees as to the accuracy of the information contained in this book and in some cases, names of people and places have been altered to protect their privacy.

© 2005 Dirk T. Dieters. All Rights Reserved.

No part of this book may be reproduced, stored in a retrieval system, or transmitted by any means without the written permission of the author.

First published by AuthorHouse 01/24/05

ISBN: 1-4208-1921-6 (sc)

Library of Congress Control Number: 2005900415

Printed in the United States of America
Bloomington, Indiana

This book is printed on acid-free paper.

From The Author

In 1995 I began analyzing small businesses. Since then I have spent time with about a thousand people who owned a $1-10 million business. By 2002 I had logged over 1000 flights, worked in 44 states and met with owners of every shape and size, race, creed and sex. It fascinated me that despite their diverse industries; their problems were very similar.

Their business was not the same business that they had started. The clients or customers were different, their goods or services were different, their employees were different, technology was different—but they had never really changed the way that they run the business. Countless dollars had been spent on people and equipment but next to nothing on "their management system." They were so busy fixing the symptoms of their problems that they never had time to deal with the causes of their problems. What they did not want to face was the fact that operational change had to take place—and they didn't know how to do it. Every one of these clients had done everything that they knew how to do—and that was the issue. If they had known what to do they would have done it. They needed help. That help is "The Fremont Business Operating System™ which is based upon this book.

From the mentors of The Fremont Group we wish you the best. **<u>GET OUT YOUR HIGHLIGHTER AND ENJOY THE BOOK!</u>**

Dirk Dieters, JD, Owner of *THE FREMONT GROUP*

www.the-fremont-group.com

This book is dedicated to my wife. Moira has been unwavering in her support—even when it was probably not justified. For all she has endured, thank you.

And to Ron Mills who has stood behind me at every turn, often sacrificing his own interests for our cause.

Table of Contents

From The Author v

Preface 1
    Growth 6

Introduction 9

Chapter One – Making Money is NOT optional 21
    Profit Plan 24
    What if Ron's company is losing money? 25
    The Plan 30
    So I'll just get a computer to solve my problems… 32
    Goals 34

Chapter Two – Tax Accounting Done Backwards 39
    Historical vs Projected 43
    So I have a budget, now what? 47
    Engineering Profit 50
    There is profit and then there is cash 51
    What you can afford and when you can afford it 51
    Profit Controls 54
    Equipment and Inventory 57

Chapter Three – Passing Out The Hats 61
    Quantitative analysis of functionality 64
    Incentives and Accountability 67

Chapter Four – People Buy From People 85
    Break even 92
    Customer service is also sales 93
    Bidding, Estimating and Pricing 94

Chapter Five – It's Not What You Make It's What You Keep 101
    Financing 104
    Inability to sell the business 105

Chapter Six – Are We Having Fun Yet? 107
    Owning a job 108
    Owning a business 109

Epilog 111

Appendix I 113

Appendix II - Worksheets 115

The Fremont Group 121

End Notes 123

"It is not the critic who counts, not the man who points out how the strong man stumbled, or where the doer of deeds could have done better. The credit belongs to the man who is actually in the arena; whose face is marred by the dust and sweat and blood; who strives valiantly; who errs and comes short again and again; who knows the great enthusiasms, the great devotions and spends himself in a worth course; who at the best, knows in the end the triumph of high achievement, and how, at worst, if he fails, at least fails while daring greatly; so that his place shall never be with those cold and timid souls who know neither victory or defeat."

Theodore Roosevelt

Preface

Small businesses start as a dream. Michael Gerber in "The E-Myth"[1] very adroitly states that most businesses are started by a technician with an entrepreneurial seizure. They understand the technical side of their business—how to make their widgets—and often they understand the sales side of their business but rarely do they understand the "business of business." They have the tools that they need for production but not the tools that they need to run their business. Typically they are working for someone else and they are technically proficient at what they do. These credentials do not necessarily equip someone to run a business. Since the business that they were working for was probably run poorly, it is no wonder that they think that they can run a business better than their current boss.

When you first start your own business, you do not in fact own a business—you own a job. The job might pay well but it is a job and the issues are compounded by the fact that they are now working for someone who really doesn't know what they are doing. This is disappointing to the person who thought that by starting their own business they would no longer have a job. The job might pay well but basically the owner is performing the same tasks that he did when he worked for someone else.[2] When you have a job, your income is determined by the work that you do. People have liked what you did in the past and when they find out that you are now working on your own, they hire you based upon their past relationship. You continue to do good work and continue to attract new customers but soon you reach the point that you have more work than you can do yourself—the moment of truth. A transition is now required—a transition that many owners never accomplish. In order to do the new work you have to hire employees—now the trouble starts. How do I get other people to do things the way I want them to? The guy with a pick-up truck and a rake who has attracted landscaping work now has to hire someone else to go to the jobs. How do you find employees? How do you train them? How do you control them? How do you maintain the level of quality that you have given these customers yourself? All of these questions haunt the expanding business owner. Many never are able to make the transition and fall back to "doing it themselves." These people are severely limited in their potential and never accomplish their dreams.

Do you want to own a job or do you want to own a business? Think seriously about this question. If all you want is a job, this book is probably not for you. If you choose to own a business you must take on a new job—the job of managing people to produce the results that you determine. If you can accomplish this your income potential increases exponentially. Your income is no longer limited to what you can produce. Your income derives from causing other people to produce the result that you want. Once you have figured out how to manage people, the really good owners then make another transition—you learn to <u>lead</u> people who do the managing. But choosing to run a business means that you have to commit yourself to <u>running</u> the business and for most people it means <u>learning how</u> to run the business.

Once a person grows comfortable with the fact that they have to have employees and is dealing with this reality, the real opportunity appears. This is the transition that only a small percentage of business owners actually achieve. This transition from owning a job to owning a business is the subject of this book. When you own a business you have the potential to earn money in two ways—compensation for the services that you are providing to the business and through the profit disbursed to ownership. Your potential compensation for the services that you provide the business is limited to the actual value added from the tasks that you perform. The potential compensation through the disbursement of profit due to ownership is limited only by your imagination. True entrepreneurship is the building of a business with profit potential, not buying a job.

Just as the owner of the business goes through an evolution, so does the business itself. In the first phase of the business' evolution all problems can be solved by more sales. Since the business was probably undercapitalized to begin with and since expenses exceed the owner's estimates cash flow becomes critical. In this start-up stage if you don't have sales growth you die. Owners become obsessed with getting the next deal so there is cash coming in. Eventually the business becomes good at generating revenues and has more cash coming in than the owner ever imagined. The owner had always assumed that if he did this much volume that he would be rich but in fact he is making less than he did when the company was smaller! In this second phase the emphasis shifts from cash flow to cash retention. How can we keep more of the money that is going through here? This is when the company matures and makes better use of management tools—budgets, cash flow forecasts, AR procedures, accountability and productivity tools, etc. This is also the first phase of the business' evolution that requires bringing in outside expertise.

The evolution of the business creates a triangle—on the first side of the triangle is the need for sales and cash flow, on the second side is the need for cash retention and controls, but it all rests on the third side of that triangle. Even after generating sales and then becoming effective at cash retention the owner reaches a point that he must also maintain a certain acceptable level of quality of life. You can't work 70 hours a week forever. You can't ignore your personal, family and health issues forever. Balancing your personal quality of life with the needs of the business is an equally important pillar.

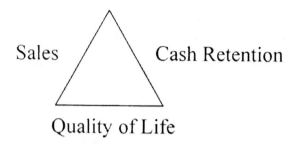

While in the sales mode every problem of the business can be solved by getting the next sale. The company is probably cash strapped and the cash that will come in from the next sale will "solve all of the problems." In order to survive the owner learns how to sell—there is no choice. However the obsession with bringing in the next sale often times continues into later getting more sales believing that the sales and marketing function of their business is what needs to be fixed. In fact the business couldn't have survived if they didn't know how to sell—the problems often lie in making enough money off of the sales that they already have. In the vast majority of companies that I go into, the owner initially believes that their problem is in sales, however after close examination that is seldom the case.

The company has often moved from the sales mode to either the cash retention mode or the quality of life mode. In the cash retention mode the company has lots of sales but no money. I ask owners, "when you started this business if I told you that you would have your current level of sales and no money, you would think that I was crazy wouldn't you." In this mode, it isn't more sales that you need, it is flypaper. All this money is going through the business but it isn't sticking. You need to make some stick. Corporate flypaper consists of basic financial tools—budgets, cash flows, collections procedures,

In the third and final stage of your business' development, you have a successful business that is generating sales and retaining cash but the personal rewards are lacking. You are working too many hours, not making enough money, or under excessive stress. The quality of life of the owner is critical to the continued success of the enterprise. If you are not having fun, you won't continue to do your job and the company will suffer from lack of leadership.

There is only one reason for your business to exist and that reason is to make your life better. Anything that is making your life better needs to be built upon, anything that is making your life worse needs to be changed or eliminated. How does your business make your life better? How does your business make your life worse? Put them on opposite sides of a sheet of paper. Then as you meet Ron and journey with him, pay particular attention to the areas that you have identified.

The purpose of this book is to open the eyes of the small business owner to the potential of their own business. Open their eyes to the changes that have to be made in order to realize the benefits of the years of "sweat equity" that they have invested. Owning your business has created only an opportunity, transforming that opportunity into a real return is the challenge.

Every business is a start-up. Older businesses are merely start-ups with a history. The size and profitability is determined by the owner. If you already own a successful business you understand that you have been successful for three reasons—you understood the technical side of the business, you have been completely committed to the success of the business and have made the sacrifices that were necessary, and you were a bit lucky. Luck plays a role. Many good businesses have failed due to bad luck or timing. Many marginal businesses have temporarily prospered due to being in the right place at the right time.

There is no "magic wand." There are only basic business practices. Those basic business practices performed properly merely reduce your reliance upon luck—but it can never be eliminated. These concepts are presented in the context of a start-up but they apply equally well to existing businesses.

Your history gives you an advantage. You are better able to make predictions of the future due to your experience in the past. This enables you to take these concepts and implement them faster and more effectively. However regardless of whether your business is a start-up or a mature company, the principles are the same. There is no magic wand. There are only basic business principles and the successful companies implement these basic business principles just a little bit better than the unsuccessful companies. In most cases these principles are analogous to the rules of physics—you are not unique and every one of them will apply to you. If you have been successful (or was it lucky?) despite not utilizing some of these principles than I congratulate you and urge you to change before gravity returns to you earth. As we all know, it is a lot more fun going up than it is going down.

Growth

As a small business owner you must recognize the fact that it is much more difficult to run your business than it is a large company—who is more likely to go out of business, you or General Motors? Small businesses cannot survive a series of bad decisions, nor can they survive extended time without proper controls. Many business owners are afraid of the "risk" involved in growth when in fact the real risk is in staying small. Businesses reach a comfort level of sales. Growth becomes stifled because the owner knows (on some level) that their systems, procedures and controls cannot profitably process additional sales. Think of the absurdity of a customer offering you money and you saying, "no thanks, I don't want to work hard enough to create the systems, procedures and controls required to profitably process your work." You as an owner have failed to adapt the way you do business to accommodate growth.

Growth may not be required for the owner—the owner might like things as they are—but growth is required to remain healthy. If the organization is not growing, the better

Minding My Own Business

employees will look elsewhere for more opportunity. You simply cannot stay the same.

Most of the time your satisfaction comes down to money. If you currently own a small business do this calculation:

> What was your average net profit percentage before taxes for the past two-three years? (Don't kid yourself!)
>
> _____% (1)
>
> What SHOULD your net profit percentage have been?
>
> ___% (2)
>
> What were your annual sales last year?
>
> $_____ (3)
>
> What SHOULD your sales have been last year?
>
> $_____ (4)
>
> What is your average gross profit percentage?
>
> _____% (5)

Compute this formula (it is not as difficult as it looks):

(2) minus (1) the remainder times (3) then add to that result:

(4) minus (3) the remainder times (5) times 80%.

((2-1)*3)+((4-3)*5*.8) = THE AMOUNT OF MONEY THAT YOU ARE LEAVING ON THE TABLE EVERY YEAR.

The concept is simple. You are first computing your "lost profit" or the difference between your current profit and the amount of profit that you believe that you should make. Then you are adding to that amount 80% of the gross profit on the difference between your actual sales and the amount that you believe that your sales should be. This is the money that your business is currently leaving on the table.

How much are you leaving on the table? Would that money make your life better? Then meet Ron and figure out how to get it.[3]

Introduction

Ron is a successful business owner. Our story relates back to when Ron was in the formative stage of his business. He was working for Acme and thought that he could make more money by working for himself. To start his business he had to work his way through all of the fundamentals of management. He was lucky—he had help. 70% of all businesses fail in the first 5 years and of those that remain, 70% of those don't last the next ten years. The lessons that he learned then still apply to his current operations. So let's flash back to five years ago.

Ron wants to start his own business. He has always talked about it but has never done it. He was good at what he was doing at Acme and assumes that he can run a business better than the people that he has seen do it. How hard could it have been for a high-paid CEO to lose millions of dollars in a quarter? Ron feels like he could have run that business and lost a million less! Ron has also seen small businesses run by people with absolutely no clue. Yet some of the clueless are making more money than Ron so why shouldn't he give it a whirl?

So Ron decided to take the plunge. He has given his notice and he feels ready. He is excited. His wife is proud. The kids are oblivious. It seems like the entire world believes that he is doing the right thing. His anticipation seems to make his present situation at Acme even worse. Cancer of the attitude has sunk in. Ron knows the industry, he knows his customers, he knows how to produce a quality product—the rest is simple, right? The big day has come. They gave him a nice party after work yesterday and now he is on his own. Ron awakes with a slight hangover and rolls over towards the window. He notices that even without the security and routine of his old job, the sun actually comes up at the same time. The kids still go to school. His wife still leaves for her work.

Everything is the same except Ron. He never knew how quiet the house was. In a panic he thinks, "What do I do now?"

For years Ron has been employee but not today. He doesn't have a job. He knows that the people at work will survive without him—shoot, six months from now they might not even remember him! After he gave his notice his boss found a replacement within a day. He thinks about going back to visit but quickly changes his mind. For years Ron has been told what he should do all day but not today. Today he gets decide for himself how to spend his time. At Acme Ron had a job. He knew exactly what he was responsible for but today that isn't so clear. What is Ron's new job? What is Ron responsible for? Ron now owns his own business. He is the chairman of the board of directors—for that matter he is the board of directors! He is the chief executive officer and he is the sole employee. He is the salesman and would be the janitor but he doesn't yet have an office. Mostly he is overwhelmed.

So Ron gets out of bed, gets dressed and decides that first he should go to breakfast. Nothing like food to clear your mind—and besides he could run into Grace. At the counter of the local diner he orders without even noticing the man sitting next to him. Sipping his coffee he waits for his eggs—over easy with hash browns. Finally the man next to him speaks. "You have either run away from home or are starting your own business." Ron is startled. "It is the "deer-in-the-headlights" look that I once had" he continued. "Well you are right—I have quit my job and I am starting my own business—you really knew that?" The man was silent. Nothing more was said until Ron's mouth was full of greasy hash browns. "I am leaving today but give me your email address. You need my help. My name is Tom—that's all you need to know." Not really knowing why, Ron scribbled his email address on the napkin without speaking slid it around the wet spot on the counter to Tom. "I will be in touch" Tom muttered as he rose to leave. "You need help." Ron finished breakfast and

Minding My Own Business

went back home. His chance meeting with Tom had left him confused and somewhat irritated. Without waiting to see if Grace was working, he called his lawyer from his cell phone and scheduled a meeting for that afternoon.

Ron enjoyed meeting with his lawyer. The view of the city from the conference room made him feel like Donald Trump. In his heart he knew that he was only a little guy starting a business and that William was only seeing him because he was his brother-in-law but the view and the leather chairs always had their designed effect. The meeting was short—William had a big case to prepare for and he also knew that Ron wasn't going to pay for his time. Ron would be incorporated within a week. They would have to meet again later to really discuss things. He knew that he should be incorporated and it felt good to be the new president of his corporation. It seemed to make everything real.

> **Incorporation law is controlled by the states. Many people confuse the reasons for incorporation with their tax status that is controlled by the IRS Code of the Federal Government. The purpose for incorporation is to avoid personal liability. A sole proprietor or a partnership results in unlimited personal liability. Corporations can incur their own tax liability (C Corporation) or can "pass through" the tax liability to the owners (S Corporation). As a general rule every business should be incorporated (or an LLC) and if you are losing money you should be an S Corporation, if you are making money you should be a C Corporation.**
>
> **HIGHTLIGHT 1**

That evening Ron went on line. As he was deleting the viagra ads and the people trying to provide him a home mortgage he saw an unfamiliar message—to be the first of many. He read Tom's first email quickly.

"Had some time at the airport and thought I would drop you a note. By now you have probably met with your lawyer. By incorporating a business a new entity is created. This entity is actually separate from you personally. We will talk more about that later. For now remember that the reason your business exists is to make your life better. If you were larger a board of directors would determine what must be accomplished in order to make the shareholder's lives' better. In your company you have the responsibility of determining the direction and goals of the company. Your plan must address four objectives:

1. You must consistently increase shareholders value of the company;

2. Deliver to the shareholders a minimum mandatory percentage of profit;

3. Maintain the quality and the integrity of the company; and

4. Grow.

Since you are the sole shareholder, you are delivering profit to yourself. You must determine the amount of that minimum mandatory percentage of profit and you must create a clear statement of what it means to "maintain the quality and the integrity of the company." So spend this evening determining those things and email back to me three things: (1) what must be accomplished in order to make your life better; (2) what is the required minimum mandatory percentage of profit that you must achieve; and (3) what it means to "maintain the quality and integrity" of your company.

I will be flying all night and will check my email tomorrow afternoon."

Tom

Ron was stunned. Who was this guy? He doesn't know me. He doesn't know my business. What is he up to? He turned off the computer. "Honey, something weird is happening."

Minding My Own Business

> **THE OWNER MUST PRODUCE THESE RESULTS:**
>
> 1. **Consistently increase shareholder value of the company;**
> 2. **Produce a pre-determined percentage of profit;**
> 3. **Maintain the quality and integrity of the company; and**
> 4. **Grow.**
>
> **HIGHTLIGHT 2**

Ron's wife Judy looked up from the television. "Did you say something?" "I met a guy at the diner this morning—it was weird." "What were you doing at the diner? That's where Grace works—we've talked about her…" "I just stopped there for some breakfast and I won't again—anyway this guy was sitting next to me. He knows just by looking at me that I was starting my own business—weird—and then he took my email address and said that he would help me."

"Grace wasn't there was she?" "No Grace wasn't there—you're missing the point. This guy just knew that I was starting a business. And now I get an email from him." "Does he seem dangerous?" "No." "What did he say?" "He gave me an assignment." "What do you mean an assignment?" "He wants me to write out some stuff about my business and email it back to him." "Why would he do that? Is he trying to steal your ideas?" "I have no idea. He wants a response by tomorrow."

Neither spoke for a minute. Finally Judy stood. "Does he make any sense?" "Well sort of. He wants me to write out what must be accomplished in order to make my life better; something about profit and something about integrity of the company."

"Haven't you done that yet?" "Honey I just met with the lawyer." "Well why don't you talk to your Dad—he was really successful in his business and…" "You know I don't talk to Dad—especially about business." Ron was getting annoyed.

"Dad and I have a hard time. Probably the most successful businessman I know and he wouldn't help anybody—you know we tried."

"Well I guess that is between you and your Dad. He did build a business and then successfully sold it—by the way we got letters from both of them today--in the same envelope, your Mother said something about him liking the new golf course. I didn't look at your Dad's."

"Must be nice to get to the point where you have money and can just play golf." Ron's stare out the front window paused the conversation. "Well if that's what you want, how do you plan to get to that point," Judy challenged. "Right now I think we can last six months but then you know we're in trouble." Ron sighed as he logged back on line. "I'm going to send this guy a response." It was a half-hearted effort.

"I don't know why you are doing this but here goes. My life would be better if I had lots of money and played golf; I want to make 50% profit and I want a quality product."

The message was sent with authority and Ron went to bed. It was an uneasy sleep. It had rained the night before and the humidity had never left.

The next morning Ron headed out the door to rent some office space. "A company needs an office" he had told Judy but he was a little unsettled when she had asked him what he would be able to afford. "Does that matter? I know what I need" he had replied. Everything he had looked at seemed expensive. Discouraged, he returned home without signing anything. He had forgotten his reply to Tom's email but quickly remembered it when he logged on to do an on-line search for more available space.

"You've got mail."

"I received your reply. It was pathetic. If you really want your business to work you have to work at making it work. If I

don't receive a serious reply in the next 24 hours you are on your own—and good luck.

You said that you want to make money—how much? What will you do with it? Is that what your wife wants? Why are you starting this business? You want 50% profit—and the people in the Middle East want peace—you can't achieve 50% profit—what would be realistic and attainable? And this bit about "quality product" what does that mean? How will you know if it is a quality product? Get back to me with some real work and we can continue. Right now you are no where near ready to start your business and that office space you are talking about will be useless.

And by the way—golf is a good walk spoiled."

Tom

Ron was speechless. He wanted to be mad but this stranger had hit a nerve. He was right and Ron hated the fact that he was right. He knew that he was at a critical moment in the short life of his business. He had to make a decision, should he invest the time in planning or just get to work? He had work lined up and didn't want to take the time to do the planning that Tom was leading up to. It might mean that he would have to delay bringing in the money that he knew he needed. He went back to the diner and made a mental note not to tell Judy that he was going to see Grace.

Grace was wearing the white outfit that he liked and she hated. Somehow talking with Grace always helped him make sense of what he was doing but Judy had a different take on the situation. Ron knew that Judy had a very different image of Grace—if she ever met her it would change. Grace was old enough to be Ron's mother but for some reason he allowed Judy to think otherwise. He had spent countless hours over cheeseburgers and apple pie during the past six months when he was trying to decide if he should quit his job. He knew that Judy didn't believe that all he was doing was eating and talking but the extra fifteen pounds seemed to be his alibi. In fact what he liked about Grace is that she didn't talk much and it gave him time to think things out.

"Hi Grace" he said as he sat in his familiar seat and picked up the menu that he knew by heart.

"Judy knows you're here?" she challenged as she placed a glass of water on the counter between them. "No and she isn't going to. I just need to talk some more. Do you remember the guy who sat next to me at breakfast yesterday?" "Sure Ron, I remember everyone who comes in here—you want his social security number?" was the sarcastic response. "No seriously—you remember him?" "No, can't say that I do. I hardly saw you. It was really busy with the convention in town."

"Well, anyway. He knew that I was starting a business and now he is sending me emails." To his pleasure Grace didn't reply but her controlled smile seemed to be hiding something. "He wants me to start writing out some things about my business and I know that it will take a lot of time."

"What do you think would be the best thing to do? I want to listen to Tom, but I want to get to work now—I have people ready to place orders."

"You have answered your own question. When you are the owner you can't always just do what you want. You have to do what is right. You have to do what is right and not what is easy—I've told you that before big man. And I was taught by the best." Grace then turned and moved on to wait on table 15. Ron sat another minute but before Grace could return he put down his water and headed towards the door. She was right.

"Now that is more like it. You have done a very good job of defining what must be accomplished in order to make your life better. Your analysis of the required minimum mandatory percentage of profit is slightly flawed but certainly a good

enough point to start from and you obviously know what it means to "maintain the quality and integrity" of your company. We are going to work together well. Now you must also understand your new responsibilities. This is critical both in new and in mature businesses. You must devise a plan. You have told me why the business is here but now you have to figure out how you are going to do it! Some owners are successful despite not even knowing what their job is. That only makes them lucky. Lucky is good. Napoleon was asked what trait he wanted in his generals—he responded, "I want them to be lucky." Even though luck is good—reliance upon luck is not. Your plan must address your six responsibilities as an owner:

1. *You must cause the business to make a minimum mandatory amount of profit.*

2. *You must create cost controls to assure that that minimum mandatory amount of profit is actually produced.*

3. *You must do something with your people. You must create an organizational structure that is focused upon the enforcement of the cost controls that you have established so that the minimum mandatory amount of profit is produced.*

4. *You must sell—externally and internally.*

5. *You must keep the money that you make and not expose it to needless risk or taxation.*

6. *You must have fun doing it.*

Not only must you develop this plan, you must implement it. I have to get to the beach while there is still sun. When I get back in I'll send you another email."

Tom

This time Ron was excited with the reply. "What I sent him was good—I put a lot of work into it" Ron said to himself. It was satisfying to Ron to know that he was starting to walk down a path that seemed right. He was no longer skeptical of Tom—he knew that this was what he should be doing. Ron closely examined these six responsibilities and started putting together a complete Strategic Plan to address each even before Tom wrote back.

> **To cause the business to produce a minimum mandatory percentage of profit, the owner must:**
>
> 1. **Identify that minimum mandatory percentage of profit;**
> 2. **Create cost controls designed to produce that minimum mandatory percentage of profit;**
> 3. **Create an organizational structure that enforces the costs controls;**
> 4. **Sell (internally and externally);**
> 5. **Create and maintain tax and risk avoidance plans; and**
> 6. **Must have fun.**
>
> **HIGHTLIGHT 3**

Ron thought back to Acme. Who was responsible for making a minimum, mandatory percentage of profit there? Acme was not that large—probably $30-40 million in sales and was owned by the O'Donoghue family. Ross O'Donoghue still ran the company. Ross and his board of directors met annually to set the company's goals. Ross then worked with his managers to develop a strategy for hitting those goals. Ron had been involved in some of those meetings—they made more sense now. At those meetings Ron was told what the "numbers" were that his division had to meet. "Those numbers were derived from the determination that the board had made as to the minimum, mandatory percentage of profit!" Ron seemed to have had a revelation and didn't require an audience for his thoughts. "Now it is obvious why they used their budgets, projected their cash flow and developed the cost controls that they did—I never appreciated what they were for. I guess it wasn't just to give us something to do."

"Okay, so they knew what their minimum, mandatory percentage of profit was and they developed cost controls in the forms of budgets, cash forecasts and key numbers that we had to focus on, I guess I was a part of that organizational structure that was called on to enforce the cost controls." At Acme Ron had been responsible for reporting weekly to Mr. O'Donoghue the results of his numbers. If they were off he had to explain why. His bonus was tied to those results.

Ron thought back to his weekly division meeting. Mr. O'Donoghue attended most of them and spent his time selling Ron and his team on how Acme worked and how they could benefit from hitting the numbers. "Guess they were selling us at those meetings. I don't know anything about their risk management or tax strategies but I do know that Mr. O'Donoghue enjoyed his work and made good money. When I think about it, the reason I quit was so I could be like him!"

"I guess the rules are the same no matter what your size." Judy was walking in the door. "Hi. Come over here and sit down." Judy came over and sat in the chair next to him. "I am going to need some help. I know that you don't aren't going to work in the business but I have decided that I have to listen to Tom and really do some planning. It is going to take some time and I will need someone that I can talk to about things. Sometimes I will just need to talk so that I can sort things out in my mind and sometimes I will want your input so that I can see other sides of issues. This is going to take some time but I think it is really important. Will you help me?" "Ron of course I will but don't expect me to understand all of these things." "I don't—but we are in this together and I need your help." "Then let's start." Judy smiled, took his hand and pulled him towards the bedroom. "Seems like a good way to start!"

Chapter One – Making Money is NOT optional

Ron is Responsible for causing the business to make a minimum mandatory percentage of profit.

<u>Chapter outline</u>
1. **Control of Profit**
    a. **Basic accounting principles**
    b. **Financial Statements (Income Statement & Balance Sheet)**
2. **Profit Plan**
3. **Strategic Planning**
4. **Leadership**
5. **Use of the Computer**
6. **Goals**

"Everyone knows that the objective of a business is to earn of a profit," Ron said to Judy who was starting dinner and not really listening. "I guess what I don't understand is the extent that I actually control that profit." The concept that he could "control" his profit had been mentioned by Tom in his last email and had been haunting Ron ever since. Earlier this morning Ron had gone to the library and checked out the business books that Tom had listed. He picked up the basic accounting book and read until he fell asleep. When he awoke Judy was cooking. He reread his notes. "Money that comes into the business from sales is called revenue."[4] "Revenue, sales—that is simple enough honey—that is simply counting the money that comes in the door." Ron read on, "in order to produce revenue a business has direct costs. A direct cost is a cost that (in theory) the business would not have if they didn't produce the revenue. In other words, a contractor would not purchase materials if he didn't have the job. He wouldn't pay field labor for a job that didn't exist. Labor and materials are the most common forms of direct costs."[5] "Okay, so your direct costs are the costs of actually doing the jobs." Judy chimed in, "So are you a direct cost?" Ron replied quickly, "as long as I am doing the work. I guess what I really want is to hire other people to be the direct costs and then I will become part of the overhead." "Are direct costs good or bad?" "Well in a way they are good. If you don't have direct costs then you aren't producing any revenue. And you better have revenue!" "So if overhead is bad why do you want to be overhead?" Judy seemed confused and Ron didn't have a quick answer.

"Let me go on." Ron was reading from his notes. "You subtract from your revenues your direct costs to obtain your gross profit." "I guess what really matters is gross profit." "So gross profit is what you really get to use?" "Basically yes. If I buy a widget for $10 and sell it for $12 then I have $2 of gross profit. I really only get to use the $2. That $2 I can apply to overhead or keep as profit." "Or give it to me?" Judy smiled at the thought.

Ron ignored the comment and went on. "What I have to do is control my direct costs so that I end up with as much gross profit as possible and also control my overhead so that the money goes to profit." Ron read on, "A company will have both profit and expense controls—profit controls deal with direct costs, expense controls deal with overhead."

"From your gross profit you subtract your overhead to arrive at your net profit. From your net profit you must purchase your new assets, pay your taxes, retain cash for the future and pay down your debt therefore net profit is not optional. Every business has a certain minimum mandatory level of net profit that it requires in order to remain viable—seems simple enough but how do you determine that minimum mandatory level of profit for your business?" Judy gave him a look that made it clear she had no idea of what he was talking about. "So what are the financial statements that your accountant does?" She asked.

Minding My Own Business

Ron knew he had an audience. "You want to know the basics?" The pride in his voice left her no choice but to say yes and resign her to a lecture. "You get two things in your financial statements—an Income Statement and a Balance Sheet." "What's the difference?" "Look over on the wall Judy, what do you see?" "A picture of us on the beach—Cabo." "Right, and what do you see in that picture?" "Well, I see us." "Right again—the two of us, sand, three sailboats in the background—you see the things that were there at the moment that the picture was taken." "Right." "What would be different if instead of a camera it was a video that was taken for five minutes?" "Well, I'd see the people who came by and the silly looks you were giving that girl on the beach." "Perfect—you would see the activity that took place during the period that the video camera ran. That is the difference between the Income Statement and the Balance Sheet. The Balance Sheet is the snapshot—the things that are there at a specific moment of time. The Income Statement is the activity that took place in the business over the period of time that you choose."

Some terms to remember:

- **BUDGET is a financial plan designed to produce a desired result.**
- **PROFIT CONTROLS are controls and reports to monitor direct costs.**
- **EXPENSE CONTROLS are controls and reports to monitor overhead.**
- **GROSS PROFIT is the amount made after the direct costs of the job.**
- **NET PROFIT is the profit after overhead is subtracted.**
- **PROFIT PLAN is how you plan to use your net profit.**
- **CASH FLOW is the money "flowing" through the company.**

> - **CASH FLOW is not the same as PROFIT.**
> - **ASSETS are the things that you own.**
> - **LIABILITIES are what you owe.**
> - **SHAREHOLDERS EQUITY is the difference between Assets and Liabilities.**
>
> **HIGHTLIGHT 4**

"Okay, so which one do you look at?" "Most of the time you look at the Income Statement because it has more to do with operations—it tells you the sales, the cost of the sales and overhead—the things that we have been talking about and the things that you must constantly control but the Balance Sheet is also important because it shows Shareholder's Value and a lot of the things that you need to know about the general health of the business. Have I confused you?" "Some, but it seems to make sense. Probably would make more sense over a glass of wine." Judy got up and went to the refrigerator.

Profit Plan

The next morning after breakfast Ron moved into his home office and went to work in his boxers. The kids had left for school, Judy had gone to work and the house was quiet. "I know that this business can make money but I don't want to be greedy. I want to be fair to my customers but I know that I have to make money too. How much money do I have to make." He went to the computer and opened Tom's next email.

"A profit plan is your first step. A profit plans starts by identifying how much will have to be spent on new assets, debt payments, cash retention and taxes. Although you are just starting the business, the same is required of existing businesses. Each one of these four items is critical.

Every year a business must invest in new assets. If you don't think so, ask your family to go for a year without the purchase of any new clothes, cars, appliances, or other purchases. You might last a while, but all you are doing is deferring the expenditure. A list must be made of all the new asset purchases that will be required for the next year. If a list would be impossible, at least an estimate of the amount of the expenditures is required[5]*. How much will we have to invest this year in new assets? If the company has debt, the retirement of that debt is paid "after tax." How much do you want to "buy down" your debt this year? Often overlooked is cash retention. If you plan to always operate your business with no cash then this is not necessary, however the folly of 25 year-old businesses with no cash reserve is the result. How much cash do we want to retain annually? Lastly, we have to pay taxes. We will attempt to minimize those taxes however they still have to be paid. In existing businesses this amount is easier to estimate, however even in a start-up some amount must be "penciled in." The sum of these four expenditures is the minimum amount of profit that must be produced. So now Ron, how much do you need and how do you plan to produce it?*

I'll be at the pool for the afternoon."

Tom

Ron made a list of the new assets that he would want to purchase in the next year. He added to it the amount that he would have to pay back on his loan, something for taxes and then the amount of cash that he wanted to add to the business next year. The amount surprised him as it was a lot more than he thought it would be. "So this is the amount of profit that we need. Guess it really is the minimum, mandatory amount that Tom was talking about."

What if Ron's company is losing money?

A panic set in on Ron. "I know that I will make money but some businesses lose money. What if I am losing money instead of making it? Take a breath—let's examine this logically. When a company is losing money it can only be for one of three reasons. The company either has an ineffective plan, the organizational structure is not delivering the plan or it is failing to effectively monitor its results."[7] When all else fails, remember the axiom, "when you are in a hole, quit digging." "I guess I need to first set a limit to the hole. Judy and I have agreed to the amount of money that we can put into this—if I lose it I will have to pull the plug. In the meantime I am comfortable that my plan is sound. I need to focus on executing that plan—getting people to deliver my results and make sure that I know they are doing it."

Then he recalled what his brother-in-law turned lawyer had told him—or was it Grace? "When you started this business you gave birth. The company is just like a person. Like your other employees the company needs a paycheck. The company's paycheck is its profit. Your employees would quit if you treated them like you treat your company. They need to know how much they are going to make and when they are going to make it so that they can plan. They have to pay old bills, acquire new assets, put away money for the future and pay their taxes. The company has to perform these exact same functions. It has to have a planned profit so that it can pay old bills, acquire new assets, put away money for the future and pay its taxes. If you don't pay the company it will quit. Not making money cannot be an option!" "That was Grace—she was talking about her diner. She is right. The business absolutely needs the minimum, mandatory profit or it will quit."

Time for a break. Ron picked up the letter addressed to him from his Father that had come yesterday. He had been meaning to read it but putting it off. Ron's father was a very successful businessman. Ron assumed that Dad wasn't really happy with his decision to go out on his own, after all Dad had once been on the Board of Directors of Acme! He had started businesses, run businesses and sold businesses and he always seemed to be in control. He sent out letters like he was sending company memos.

It was a copy of a magazine article. "**Your success is limited to the excuses that you are willing to accept.** When an employee comes to you with his excuse for not meeting the predetermined level of performance your leadership immediately comes into play. You must listen to what they say and then determine if you have been given an excuse or a reason for nonperformance. The difference between an excuse and a reason is—an excuse isn't true! The nice part of being the boss is that you get to decide what the truth is. There are occasions when there can be a reason—a legitimate, true reason why performance could not be accomplished. That is why you have to listen to the employee. When a true reason is put forth you must then modify your plan. The performance that you had planned cannot be met. However it is far more common that your employee (or you yourself) will come to you with an excuse instead of a reason. If you accept the excuse you have limited your success. More likely you should inform them that you do not accept their excuse and that you still expect the pre-determined performance. Employees are like children and they will push. If you give in you have turned the company over to them."

Judy walked in and he didn't even ask why she had come back home. He turned and muttered in her direction. "Dad never writes normal letters. He even sent out notes at Christmas that included a quiz at the end. If only he would share some things with me about business that would make me money…" The article seemed to drone on and Ron started to skim.

"Leadership requires decisiveness.[8] If the employees feel reluctance on your part to take action, they loose respect for you as a leader. The company's direction must be clearly defined, the systems and procedures clearly communicated, and company policies must be firmly and fairly enforced.

"Mistakes can usually be corrected later; the time lost in not making a decision can never be retrieved."[9]

"A leader, then, is a person who is orientated toward results more than power or social relations....the results-orientated leader does not dictate the methods for achieving the results and, moreover, does not need to claim the victories as his own."[10]

Ron skipped the rest and pulled out another newspaper clipping that his father had attached. Ron Battles, Director of the Small Business Development Center of Everett, Washington[11] was asked to name the biggest mistake in small business. He stated, "Being slow to adapt to business conditions even though you think you're fast…. I had to do something but if I had done it a year earlier, I would have been a lot further along. **As a business owner, if there's a decision to be made you have to make it quickly. If you don't make it you lose the timing of that decision.**"

The letter concluded with Dad writing, "Employing people creates a stewardship. You owe it to your employees to provide them with a secure company, opportunities for growth, and respect. Many owners misinterpret this stewardship and do not make the hard decisions. What they often do is cause the entire company to suffer in an attempt not to "hurt" one of them. Your job requires you to deliver to the shareholders a pre-determined profit, maintain the quality and integrity of the company, and to grow. Ron you must do your job as well as you expect others to do theirs. Leadership is having a plan and getting your people to focus upon their part of the plan."[12] "At least Dad wrote some of this!"

Ron put down the letter. "Dad didn't even sign it. Actually he doesn't even write this stuff he just copies it from the stuff that he reads. I wish that he would quit it and help me as much as Tom does," he said to Judy and he turned his attention to his legal pad. "What does all of this leadership stuff have to do with our situation? I swear…" On the pad he had written the following questions:

- How much money are we planning on making this year?
- What will be required in sales according to the plan?
- What will be required in Gross Profit according to the plan?
- What overhead level is permissible according to the plan?
- Other than money, what other results must the business generate this year?

Judy interrupted his thoughts. "Guess I am as bad as your Dad—I copied this quote today. I thought it might fit in with what you are doing. It is from Teddy Roosevelt. "The best executive is the one who has enough sense to pick good people to do what he wants done, and self-restraint enough to keep from meddling with them while they do it." Ron looked at it for a while before commenting. "That does sound like Dad. Makes sense though. I guess you really have to have a plan in place before you can just turn good people loose."

The quote started haunting Ron. "Let's talk about that quote." Judy looked a little like she had gotten herself into more than she had bargained for. "The best executive…" he isn't talking about manager—executive. The executive is the leader—the owner. "has enough sense to pick good people…" which implies that he doesn't just hire he "picks" people. To pick people you have to have a criteria that you have set and match people to. "what he wants done…" which means that he knew what he wanted done ahead of time; he had a plan and knew where this person would fit <u>before</u> he even picked the person. He knows the results that he has to have that person produce. "and self-restraint enough to keep from meddling…" so he isn't going to micromanage yet to have the self-restraint not to meddle you have to know that the person is on-track at all times to produce the result that you have directed—that means effective reporting, "while they do it." That really does say a lot Judy." Judy was impressed with herself. "Teddy was ahead of his time."

The Plan

Ron went back to his computer. Tom had sent another email.

"Imagine a football coach. We all know that he has a game plan established for every game. He would lose his job if his game plan said, "If everything goes right we will only lose by a touchdown." Yet this is done in small businesses every day. The financial plan of a company is their cornerstone. How are we planning on making our pre-determined profit? What sales are required? What gross profit is required? What overhead levels are required? What is our plan for overhead absorption by profit center? Obviously your game plan must be designed so that the targeted performance produces your desired result. Once established (and the more specific the better) then it becomes the role of your Organizational Structure to focus your people on their individual results that they must produce in order to perform their part of your plan. The company's financial reporting monitors these results so that people can be held accountable and incentives established and monitors the company's progress in relation to the plan.

Every plan must address the following objectives: first it must assure that the business continue to function and stay in business for the next week, month, six months, year, etc. Second, the business must make money and third the business must grow. Any plan that does not address all of these objectives is fatally flawed. Business continuation is obvious but often overlooked. There are cycles to the business and the owner must be prepared to be able to withstand the "down" cycles. You must also identify and develop a management plan that includes key management succession *and a structure to shift reliance from people to systems to assure business continuation. No employee (owner included) should have the ability to hold the company hostage. Lastly the business must grow. This is vital not so much for your short-term return but rather it is required for retention of employees. A growing business offers more opportunity for employees and is more likely to retain the better people. Failing to grow eliminates those opportunities and causes the better people to leave—a reverse Darwinism—that is eventually fatal. Without retaining and challenging the best people succession of management is compromised.*

The function of a company's advisors is to assist them in climbing the steps to wisdom. Not every company needs a full-functioning board of directors; however every company needs to have the scrutiny of outsiders to keep them from getting "too close to the forest to see the trees." An owner who does not have any real mentors or advisors has to perform this role is on his own. He does very well within his comfort level but lacks input that could result in innovation.

Attorneys are poor advisors. They are trained in the law, not in business. If fact, they are notoriously poor businessmen. It is vital to have a strong relationship with your attorney so that the attorney is prepared to handle whatever legal issues the company might generate but do not expect operational advice from them—nor should you accept it. They do not sit in your chair and do not understand the hard choices that you must make.

CPA's are trained to do your taxes. Again they are notoriously poor businessmen. They do not come into your business and examine the operations, make attempts to understand how your industry works, or really assist you in running your business. They should be providing adequate tax advice but even that rarely happens. Your CPA makes his money by doing your taxes. If they were to provide consulting advice, they would have to stop doing your taxes due to the conflict of interest. They also have little incentive to see that you pay the minimum amount of tax. The way they lose your account is to put forth a tax plan that is disallowed on audit—therefore they only push you far enough into the "gray" so that you are happy. If almost any small business owner walked into their CPA's office and demanded that their CPA find a way to lower their taxes, the CPA would come back with a change to lower their taxes. Why don't they do it on their own? "To me, it cannot be anything other than sensible and responsible to bring a ship's pilot on board when you are steering your vessel into new and dangerous waters!"[13]

Tom

Ron needed some time for Tom's advice to sink in—this was too much to sink in at once. Judy sat down next him.

"I have to go back to work—just came back to pick up the file that I left here. You want to drive me back and keep the car?" "That would work well—I have an appointment with a computer guy and maybe that software that he is talking about will save me all of this work. He is near your office—ready to go?"

So I'll just get a computer to solve my problems...

Ron described his project to Steve who ran the local software shop. "Many people over-estimate the function of a computer system. They think that new hardware or software will solve their problems. In almost no case is this true. Let me show you something." Steve then took out a sheet of paper.

"Data is accumulated throughout the organization—invoices, time cards, purchase orders, etc. The major concern at this level is the integrity of the data. It has to be accurate. You will have to go elsewhere to make sure that you actually gather accurate data."

Minding My Own Business

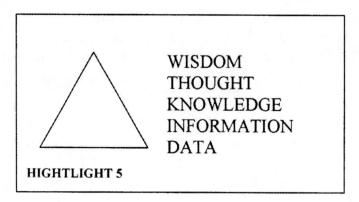

HIGHTLIGHT 5

"Information is the conversion of that data into a usable format—reports. This is the function of the computer. The computer takes data and converts it into information. It is also indiscriminate in this function—it will produce all the reports you want from the data that it is given. I can get you software that can create any reports that you want. The problem will be limiting this information to what you need, not generating it."

"Knowledge is knowing what information that you need and what to do with it. The computer cannot improve knowledge. This is the function of your advisors. Consulting deals specifically with this issue and trains you continue through the flow to wisdom."

"Thought is used to analyze the proper information and take actions in your operations that will change the data so that the information matches your desired result. Wisdom is acquired through the repetition of the process. Notice that the computer addresses only one of these steps."

It didn't take Ron long to figure out that he could go broke buying the "new and improved" software and hardware and yet none of it would take him to "knowledge" or "wisdom" and he passed on Steve's "special offer just for him" and drove home. One thing that Steve said did hit home though. Ron asked Steve what would be the best software program for his business. Steve thought for a second and said, "there is one software program that is better than any other—it clearly would be the best program for you." Ron had to ask, "and what program would that be?" Steve smiled and said, "the program that the person who has to run it likes and understands."

Ron was hoping that the computer would offer him a "quick fix" and he was somewhat disappointed. He arrived home and saw the message from Judy—she would be home late. Ron thought about the diner but wasn't in the mood. Instead he went to the refrigerator to make a sandwich. He hated it when they were out of mayo but it didn't stop him from eating two. It was time to refocus—maybe a third sandwich would help. "I think I should write out my goals" he said to the cat. The cat didn't answer.

Goals

Ron picked up a sheet that he had found years ago in his father's office. It seemed so familiar—as if he had seen it somewhere else. It was divided into a large "T." On the right side was the caption, "Long-Term Goals" and on the left side, "Short-Term Goals." "What are the long and short term goals for the business and for myself?" The cat still didn't answer. At the bottom was a notation that the "goals must be specific, measurable, attainable, realistic and timely. The clearer the destination the more likely you are to arrive there."

On the back it read, "Goals cannot however be done in a vacuum. Since they require the "cooperation" of customers to be achieved, they must also be customer orientated. The only way to achieve success is to establish goals that are customer-related. In order for anything to be achieved, a company must first please their customers. In many cases the company has not truly defined who their customers are, what they want and why they should buy it from them. Becoming a "problem-solver" for your customers is the only long-term strategy that will succeed. Who are the customers? What are the customer's needs? What can you do to solve your customer's problems? The company goals must be re-orientated to addressing these issues. If you don't, someone else will."

"So where do I start?" I suppose that first I will answer the questions on the back—why should someone buy from me instead of my competitor?" This turned out to be a little harder to answer than it seemed. It was tempting to talk about quality and customer service but everyone talks about that. Finally the cat had something to contribute—"put yourself in the position of the customer." "Did she really say that? Anyway... what would I say if I were the customer instead of me? How do I want my company to look to my customer? This is what is important."

Now the answer seemed to flow and in doing so, Ron realized where he had seen this chart before—Acme used it too! Mr. O'Donoghue had one just like it.

> **Why does the customer buy from me instead of my competitor?**
>
> **In the eyes of your customer, this is what your business is. It can be altered but it remains who you are. If you are happy with this position, make sure that it is reinforced throughout the organization and at every opportunity to the public and your customers.**
>
> **HIGHTLIGHT 6**

"One of my goals is to provide a quality product. What is "quality?" I once read that quality is the delivery of a consistent customer experience. McDonalds does not have the best hamburger however it is the same everywhere, every time. Customers equate quality with a <u>consistency</u> of customer experience—not with the best product on the market. How do you deliver quality? McDonald's people are not the best—mine are better—but their systems are much better than mine. I guess I can deduce that quality is a trait of a Systems Dependent business. It makes sense that if you are relying upon people—a People Dependent business—it is impossible to deliver a consistent customer experience.

SMART GOALS

Make your goals "SMART"

- SPECIFIC
- MEASURABLE
- ATTAINABLE
- REALISTIC
- TIMELY

(Attainable and realistic might be the same thing but SMAT doesn't sound as good!)

HIGHLIGHT 7

Ron wrote out his short and long-term goals (both for the business and personal). Each time he wrote one he asked himself, "how will I be able to measure results to determine if I have accomplished each goal?" "I have to write them so I can hold myself accountable."

As Ron read back his goals he seemed to have some issues—were some of the goals really "sub-goals" other ones or should they be separate. Finally Ron decided that there were really only three types of goals—the large financial goals of revenue, profit, and cash flow; the organizational goals of how he wanted the place to work; and the personal goals that he set. Within each were the actions that would be required to accomplish each broader goal. He labeled his former goals into "Goals" and "Actions." Smiling he saw some of the very statements that Acme had written out for his department.

In order to better understand what he wanted to do, Ron spent the entire next day working on a 25-word statement of

Minding My Own Business

why someone should buy from him instead of his competitor. He realized the importance of keeping this statement within the context of the Goals and Actions that he had already written. By dinner time he was both exhausted and energized.

Judy had made him promise that tonight they wouldn't talk business but he couldn't help but tell her how much better he felt from the focus he had developed by writing out his Goals, Actions and his 25-word statement. She smiled and put on the movie she had rented. Not even the "chick-flick" could dull his enthusiasm and half-way through it he added a last edit to his list.

Judy took what Ron had said about helping him seriously. The next morning was Saturday and she greeted Ron with a legal pad for breakfast. "Let's summarize where you are so far." Ron poured a cup of coffee and smiled.

"Well the focus has thus far has been on profit. I understand that I can—to some degree—control the amount of volume that the business will do and the amount of money that it will make." Judy was busy scratching down notes. "I learned basic accounting principles—which I already pretty well knew—but also about a Profit Plan. The Profit Plan dictates the minimum, mandatory amount of profit that the company must make. This had to be determined before I could start into strategic planning. You know, I used to think that the bank was the only one who wanted a business plan—now I understand that it is really for me. The strategic plan outlines what I'm going to do and how I plan to do it. I tied it to my goals which in a way tell me why I want to do it."

Toast popped up from the toaster and Ron paused his summary so that he could butter it and let Judy catch up. "Steve showed me that the computer isn't going to answer all of my questions, but I see now how important a tool it is, particularly in the generation of information."

Ron put the toast in front of Judy and sat back in his chair. She spent a few more minutes writing before she looked up. "Anything else?" she asked. Ron thought and then refilled his coffee cup. "The only other area that Tom addressed was leadership. He defines leadership as having a plan and communicating that plan to your people. I think it is a little more and that is inspiring them to accomplish their part of the plan." "I doubt Tom would be bothered by that addition" Judy added. Ron smiled and looked at the notes. "This will help. I'll add them to my notebook."

Chapter Two – Tax Accounting Done Backwards

Ron is Responsible for creating cost controls which result in the business making his minimum mandatory percentage of profit.

Chapter Outline

1. **The managerial use of accounting**
2. **Key Profit Indicators (KPI's)**
3. **Budget**
4. **Cash Forecasting**
5. **Overhead Allocation**
6. **Equipment and Inventory Controls**

"Ron, you have a limited understanding of accounting. You can hire a bookkeeper to compile information for me but you need to know the tax return that I will prepare is not a true indication of how your business runs." The meeting with the accountant was not going well. Patrick had been highly recommended. He was prompt and saw Ron on time but it was also obvious that Patrick really didn't understand how the business worked. He did seem to understand taxes. Ron had assumed that Patrick would be producing the reports and information that he wanted on a daily basis and was shocked to find out that the CPA doing his taxes actually had an ethical conflict of interests in giving managerial advice. "So you are saying that the accounting you will produce doesn't give me anything that I can really use?" Patrick was calm in his response. "I can assure you that you need to have your taxes done. What I am saying is that you will not receive from me answers as to what you can afford or when you can afford it. That is not practical. By the time that you gather the data, send it to me, allow me the time to analyze it and then send it back to you it is too late. You have to do most of that internally. You will have to track some areas—usually sales and rely upon your "gut feel" or create your own internal reports. The good news is that the more experienced you get, the more likely that your "gut feel" will be correct. The bad news is that the business easily outgrows this method and it is impossible either to delegate this management style or to transition this style to an heir or successor. Sooner or later the small mistakes become big dollars." "You aren't real encouraging Patrick." "You will figure it out." Patrick smiled and was pleased with his response. Ron felt like he hadn't heard the last from Patrick.

The ride home was short. Ron had hoped for more. It was disappointing to realize that the CPA was only really trained in doing taxes and that he knew his needs from his accounting were much greater. Ron was comforted when he saw another email from Tom. It had been nearly a week—something about no email on the cruise ship.

"I often use this analogy. "Look out of the window. Imagine that you see a young child crossing the street. A speeding car approaches and hits the child—a terrible, terrible tragedy. After you observe this event you sit down and write three letters describing the tragedy. The first letter is to your best friend. The second is to your young child and the last is to your lawyer. Each of the letters is truthful but imagine how each will be different. Your accounting also needs different kinds of "letters." The only "letter" that you currently are set up to produce is a letter that the bookkeeper will write to the CPA for the purpose of taxes. This is a very important letter but it does not provide you with what you need to run the business. Most owners recognize this deficiency but simply just don't know what to do about it. They are getting the wrong letter. Imagine how baffled the young child would be if he received the letter written to the lawyer. If you only produce this letter you will be like that confused child.

You must produce this letter for your CPA but you must also produce two more letters. The second letter is the letter to yourself generating the information that you need to know to run the business.

*Every business can be broken into 4-10 key profit indicators—KPI's. These key variables must be projected and tracked **weekly**. Why weekly? It is the attainment of these results that determines the profit of the company and that is the reason we are in business. The more that one focuses on the result that they wish to achieve, the more likely they are to achieve that result. There are no lasting religions that have people come to church once a year, or once a month, or once a quarter. A weekly focus is exponentially more likely to deliver your result. The timeliness of the information in this instance is more important than the accuracy. You will have a difficult time convincing you bookkeeper of that because their entire orientation is towards accuracy, however the purpose of these "flash reports" is not their accuracy—it is the focus that they create. If a report indicates that a number is out of the range that you have established, it then is the responsibility of the proper person to identify why and what is being done to correct it.[14] (As scary as it seems to some owners, there are variables that must be tracked daily! But learn to walk before you run.)"*

The third letter you must produce is the letter for the three outside "B" people—bankers, bonders and buyers. When you go to the bank you are making a sales call—you are trying to "sell" the bank on "buying your company" and lending you money. If you go on a sales call with a brochure that describes your company as, "not very good at what we do" and you put that in front of a customer and while asking them to buy your product I would think that you would want a new sales brochure! Yet that is what you do when you take your tax accounting to the bank! Tax accounting is designed to make your company look bad—minimize profit to minimize taxes. For bankers, bonders and buyers you need a different sales piece and it's not your managerial information. They need projections, cash flow utilizations, valuations of the business and inventory at market rather than book—things that paint a rosier picture of your business. Then you also submit the tax returns to show what a good job of tax avoidance you do! Sleep on this and respond with any questions—I've got to get to dinner.

Tom

Ron read this three times before looking up. "I see now why Patrick wasn't as helpful as I wanted him to be. He deals only with tax accounting. Ron sat back down at his computer and sent off an email to Tom.

Tom

Your email has raised two questions—first you mentioned timeliness. What do you mean by that? Second could you write some more about the role of the accountant?

Thanks

Ron

Ron couldn't wait to get out of bed. Tom's response was waiting for him.

Ron

All information produced by a company must meet four criteria: it must be timely, accurate, usable and produced at a minimum cost. Timely means that it must be delivered at a point in that acting upon the information can make a difference. If a football coach covers the scoreboard during the game and then waits until Tuesday to read the paper to find out if he has won or lost, he has not received timely information. As absurd as that sounds, that is exactly how many business owners operate. The term accurate is often misunderstood. In our context accurate means as accurate as is necessary for the purpose of the report. Accountants and bookkeepers put a very high standard upon accuracy and that is good—especially for tax purposes; however, all reports do not require that same degree of accuracy. Accountants and software completely overlook the "usable" criteria. Business owners rarely have the same level of sophistication regarding accounting as their CPA and therefore the format of the reports needs to be adjusted. This is particularly true as the reports filter down through the organization. If it is not understood, it is of no value. Lastly the information must be produced at a minimum cost. There is a cost to the production of all information and it is senseless to spend $500 to create a report that generates $100 of profit.

Historical vs Projected

Information provided by your accountant is historical information. Anything that has to be prepared and reviewed in-house, then shipped to the accountant, reviewed and compiled there and then shipped back has to be historical. Historical information does have its' place. In looking for trends, identifying where the company has been and in preparing forecasts, historical information can be very useful. However, the value of historical information diminishes in businesses with rapid change. Small businesses can double their sales in a year. They can move into new locations with completely different overhead structures. They can quickly move to different products and customers. In such an environment, historical information becomes just slightly more than an academic pursuit.

The only thing that is really relevant to the business owner is how the company stands in relation to their plan. But most owners don't even have a plan! Most owners are so sucked into the daily operations (other people's jobs) that they fail to do <u>their</u> job. Their first job is to plan. This is a constant process. Man plans and God laughs. The plan is not even intended to work; rather it is intended to create benchmarks against which the company's performance will be measured. The revision of this plan is a **constant** process, not an annual event. At least monthly, you must review your benchmarks and revise the plan. *(Obviously from this plan is generated the operational standards for the organization.) You project revenues and cost of sales—by product or department—and establish overhead using only percentages.*

Tom

Judy was getting ready for work. "What has you at the computer at 6:30 in the morning?" "Working with Tom on my accounting needs—coffee is ready." "I can smell it. This thing with Tom is working out better than you thought isn't it?" "It really is Honey. I was so skeptical at first but now it is as if he really understands what I am doing and anticipates everything that I am going through." "What are you doing next?" Judy sipped her coffee as she glanced at the paper. "Well next I have to put together a budget. It will be my financial plan for the business." Judy had already left the room and headed towards the coffee. "I'm not as good with numbers as you but I'll try to help after work." Ron smiled and opened up his spread sheet as Judy kissed him good bye to leave for work.

Ron knows that he needs a budget but he doesn't have one. It is Ron's most important management tool.

Ron went back to the accounting book. Tom had mailed it to him and calling it a "book" was generous. It was more like a collection of notes that Tom must have written. "A "budget" is a financial plan designed to produce a pre-determined result.

Sales		100%
COGS		
	Materials	30%
	Labor	30%
	Other	10%
	Total COGS	70%
Gross Profit		30%
Overhead		20%
Net Profit		10%

"I can see now that it is critical that the budget be in percentages and not dollars. Only the Federal Government can budget dollars because they are not restricted to what comes in—I am. My job is to hit two numbers—the 70% Gross Profit and the 20% Overhead. If these two numbers hit, I will hit my profit." "You talking to someone honey?" Ron thought that Judy had left and was embarrassed to admit that he had just been talking out loud. "No—it's the radio."

"I need to tie down those numbers, create systems for the constant revision of those numbers and create focus throughout the entire organization on hitting those numbers." At least Ron was now not thinking out loud. In fact he was glad that he wasn't because even Judy would assume that he had already done this.

> After you have laid out your own budget in broad numbers compare it to your historical results and the industry numbers to determine if it is realistic.
>
> **HIGHLIGHT 8**

"Judy, I need some help. Could you come here a minute and just listen to me?" "Sure, be right there, but I have to get going." "Since my job is to hit two numbers—direct costs and overhead. I will start with the assumption that I am no good—that I will not hit those two numbers." Ron made a note on his pad to read the section about Profit Plans again. "I will create a <u>Profit Plan</u> for the business based upon half of the amount of planned net profit that I think I can make. The Profit Plan determines how much will be spent on new assets, retirement of debt, retention of cash and taxes. This way the business can be relatively certain of achieving it since it is based only on half of the profit that they should be doing. This way if I achieve my full profit I can keep the second half as a bonus. That would not compromise the company as their needs have been accounted for in the first half."

"Now I see some more things--if the person who is responsible for holding the direct labor to 30% is able to do his job better and holds it to 28%, he has produced an <u>additional 2% profit</u>. This is beyond the budgeted profit and becomes the basis for an incentive.[15] One-half percent is paid to the person who produced it; one-half percent to me for managing him so effectively and one percent is paid to the company for additional assets, debt retirement, cash retention and taxes. This formula is carried through to the other key profit variables." "So that is how you determine incentives for your employees," Judy chimed in. "It sounds good to me—one for them and three for us!"

"The amount needed to fund the profit plan, when divided by .1 (the desired net profit) gives you the company's required sales for break even. Not even a sales plan can be developed without a budget!"

"If I have different profit centers one individual must be held responsible for the gross profit generation of each profit center; however the strategic plan and not a subjective standard must determine the absorption of the company overhead by profit center. "A company with more than one profit center has to determine how to allocate their fixed overhead between departments." I could call Patrick and ask how the overhead of his company should be allocated between departments but I know what he would do. What I would receive is a very competent analysis of which department utilizes what percentage of each cost—and a large bill. What I would not receive is an analysis of the strategic advantages of various overhead allocations. "The allocation of overhead by profit center is different in every business and it is one of the competitive advantages (disadvantages) of each entity." My strategic plan should determine the overhead absorption for each profit center."

"In effect, I build my income statement with each job. The sum of all of the contract prices equals the total sales. The sum of all the job costs equals my direct costs and gives me my gross profit. If I am properly estimating my sales volume and I properly estimate my overhead, I know exactly what percentage of overhead needs to go into each price."

"Overhead allocation strategies allow for companies to develop pricing strategies, competitive advantages, and growth of new divisions. In order to effectively do this, it requires that the financial statements to be properly stated and the true costs known. These are advanced strategies that separate average small businesses from those businesses committed to the next level."

"Honey, I don't understand a word of what you just said and I have to get to work." "Just give me another minute. I want to say this again out loud to make sure that I understand it. Once you know your true break even, there are some neat things that you can do. Every job has three components to its price—the direct cost of doing the job, the profit that I want to make and the allocation for overhead. My break even is the amount of sales revenues that are required to pay all of my overhead, so once I pass that break even, I have paid all of my overhead so if I want I can reduce my prices by the percentage of my overhead!" "Honey, that is exciting to you, but I need to get to work—keep on it, love you!"

Ron spent the rest of the morning playing with numbers. As numbers is one of his talents he was able to work it out to his satisfaction. He still had a number of questions and felt the call of the diner.

So I have a budget, now what?

Ron settled into his corner booth. Grace came by with coffee and a glance at the budget that Ron was working on. His papers filled the table. There were only two other people in the diner so Grace sat down and looked at the work Ron had done. He had sketched out his budget and was trying to identify the reports that he wanted to receive.

"Internal reports are generated for the purpose of monitoring the results of either an individual or of the company. It is senseless to produce reports without also producing an analysis of those results against your plan. Variance analysis indicates how the actual result varies from the plan. Why produce the report if this is not done?"

"Comparing results to last year, or last month is only valid if you want the same results as last year or last month. The relevant comparison is to your plan. You are very much moving in the right direction by starting with your budget." Ron was dumbfounded. He thought he would bounce a few things off of Grace and get mostly a free refill of his coffee in reply but her response amazed him. "How do you know all this Grace? You sound just like Tom." "Tom and I were taught by the best" she replied. "There are a half-dozen different things that I track daily here at the diner."

"Just like you have done, I start by determining the amount of profit that I want to make. You need enough internally generated information to have control of your KPI's and ultimately your profit. Most business owners do not even know that they can control their profit. Accountants do you no favors. They have beaten into the heads of business owners an accounting format in which profit is treated as a residual. Pull out your financial statements." "Grace, I don't usually bring my financial statements to lunch." "Okay, okay. Then just sketch it out on this napkin. This I how they look: on the top line is revenues followed by the cost of goods sold. These numbers are subtracted and the result is your gross profit." "Looks like my budget." "Right and wrong. Then you subtract overhead <u>and what is left over is profit.</u> Right? Wrong. This is tax accounting. This is the basis of the letter written to the CPA for the purposes of paying (or hopefully avoiding) taxes. This is not managerial accounting. That is why in your budget you put in the profit that you think you should make first and do this all backwards. Actually it is your tax accounting done backwards. If you use your tax accounting to compute your break even you will divide your fixed overhead by your gross profit percentage resulting in the company revenues needed to pay your bills. **But we are not in business just to pay our bills."** "Tom has taught me that it is my job to generate a *pre-determined profit."* "Right, if you take what is left over, that is what you will get and that is why you have to treat your profit as one of your overhead expenses for the purposes of computing break even."

"Do you know Tom—the guy that I met here—remember?" "Well we might very well have had the same teacher." "So where do I find this teacher?" "Let's just say that when the pupil is ready the teacher arrives."

Ron thanked Grace, drove back home and went back to his study. His study was actually a table in the living room that Judy constantly wanted him to clean up. It was piled with books and papers that overflowed the computer keyboard. There were glasses, pop cans and supplies spilling over to the floor. Ron dug out the accounting book. Ron examined it closely. Tom had lent him the book but it was more of a binder—certainly nothing that could be found in the library. It seemed to continue Grace's discussion. Any thoughts of cleaning up the table to surprise Judy drifted away into the text.

"On your financial statement, go to the space between gross profit and overhead. Insert the amount of profit that your Strategic Plan shows that you need to make. Now add that to your overhead and divide the result by your gross profit percentage. That is the sales volume required to really "break even." Now you can develop a sales plan." "Funny, I wanted to start with the sales plan not even knowing if it was designed to "win the game" and not to merely "lose by a touchdown." I was completely backwards." Ron had to look up to make sure that no one had heard him talking to himself.

Ron also thought back to Acme. They seemed to be obsessed by budgets—and now it made sense. The KPI's were the "numbers" that each of the managers, like himself, had been held accountable for monitoring and producing.

Engineering Profit

Another e-mail had arrived from Tom.

"Making money is so simple that most people don't understand it. If you want to make 10% profit, simply spend only 90 cents of every dollar that comes in. Anyone can figure that out. So why do so few people have a plan to do it? In producing a profit there are only two variables. First is the relationship between what you charge (price) and what it <u>actually</u> costs you to produce your product. Second is the relationship between overhead and gross revenues. You want to make money? Establish your plan to determine the required relationship between price and cost (gross profit), identify ALL of the variables that control this relationship, pick out the key ones and monitor the crap out of them. Then take out your desired net profit from the gross profit and establish the amount of overhead that the company can afford. Implement controls so that the overhead cannot exceed that level and you end up with your profit. Simple isn't it? Unfortunately 99 out of every 100 small business owners spend virtually no time focusing upon making money because they are "too busy" (doing other people's jobs). It is also overwhelming to them because their accountant and software have provided tools that are inadequate and overly complex. Those really making money are doing it despite these inadequacies and with a lot of luck. Reliance upon luck can be significantly reduced if the proper information is generated and USED.

Making money is a "no brainer."

"Tom might be getting a little carried away there!" thought Ron.

The company's income statement is built through the sum of these same actions... All of the total prices charged equal your total income; all of your job costs equal your cost of good sold. Subtract your total overhead and you have your net profit. The company's financial plan provides these target ratios and then it becomes your responsibility to run the business to meet those numbers. Obviously you must monitor the crap out of all of the variables that go into these two ratios. **This is what it means to run the company. This is what it means to "try" to make money.**

There is profit and then there is cash.

Cash management is the company's system of converting sales dollars into cash. There is no real gain from making more to spend more. The only way to acquire wealth is to spend less than you earn and retain cash. All of the money that comes in here goes back out. Cash is the most powerful asset that a company has. It is also the most ignored asset in the business. Cash should be a profit center generating between ¼ and ½ % of sales in bottom line profit. Cash is not dependent on profitability. Cash can be generated at a consistent level even during periods of decline in business. Cash management covers billing procedures, collection procedures, inventory control, purchasing procedures, fixed asset purchasing, depreciation methodology and budgeting procedures. Any of the areas mentioned can be the cause of no money in the bank. Most of the time it is a combination of all of the areas mentioned. All of these areas must be addressed if you are to have consistent levels of cash in your business."

Tom

What you can afford and when you can afford it[16]

Ron called back Patrick the accountant. "How can I really know what I can afford and when I can afford it?" Patrick paused. "I didn't tell you some things last time because you weren't ready. A Company's budget establishes what they can afford—their cash flow establishes when they will be able to afford it. The budget is merely the company's financial plan to obtain their desired result. It is obviously central to a company's success and a basic business tool. The budget is the financial model that the business must achieve in order to get your results. You don't want to run your company with "mailbox management?" "So I need to develop a Budget and a Cash Flow forecasting system?" "Right. Without an effective budget it is impossible to determine the job performance standards or have any basis for an incentive program."

Patrick loved giving advice even though he knew that he was getting a little out of his element. "The cash flow forecast allows you to make promises that you can keep. You must be able to project the company's cash position for a minimum of six weeks forward at all times. How else can you have control of your cash? This would also be a good time to talk about the "cost of growth." Whenever a business grows, you have to pay out money for labor and materials before you get paid. I am going to give you a formula that computes how much money you will need up-front in order to "finance" the amount of growth you want. Let's say you want to grow $1 million in sales next year. If your cost of goods sold is 70% you multiply the amount of anticipated growth ($1 million) by 70% then divide it by 365 (the number of days in a year) and multiply it by the number of days in your average collection rate (how fast you get paid.)[17] This tells you how much money you need up-front to finance your receivables." Ron hated it when Patrick got condescending. Maybe Grace could give him something more useable.

"You expect your employees to do their jobs; it is time that you did yours." Grace was never one to mince words. "Establish the financial plan and budget. If you don't know how to do it, get help but you have to do it. It is from the budget that you identify the results needed by each employee and create monitors and reports to track the results. No one went into business to read reports and push paper. We went into business to make money. If you want to work for your employee's wages, do their jobs. If you want to fulfill those dreams that caused you to start your business, do the owner's job." "I'll skip the pie Grace."

Grace was good at bringing him down to earth. Ron stopped at the liquor store on the way home to pick up a bottle of wine for the evening. He beat Judy home and decided that he had time to read Tom's email while the wine breathed—as if the wine they bought needed to breathe.

"Cash is king. Without it you have nothing. As long as your customers have your cash instead of you, you have nothing except the expense of producing the product. It is estimated that when your customer has the money it costs you 9% and when you have the money you can make 9% so there is an 18% swing between you having the money and your customer having the money.[18] *This is money that otherwise would be on your bottom line.*

In most businesses billing must be done daily. Weekly or monthly billing is totally unacceptable. Weekly billing adds four days to the average collection period. Monthly billing adds seventeen days to the average collection period. Time is money. The longer the time interval between billing periods, the higher the level of errors and omissions in billings. Collections must be done by telephone. Good cash management programs teach owners to pay their bills as late as possible without hurting their credit. How do you know how late you can pay your bills—you should pay the bill so that it arrives one day prior to the day that they call. The reverse is true in collection. The earlier the telephone calls the earlier the payment. Collections begin at the time of the sale. Reduction of the collection period can generate significant cash for the business causing significant bottom line impact. A company must have standards for their receivables, must have people responsible for obtaining those standards that have been given the authority to control their result, must monitor the result and must hold those people accountable for those results."

Tom

"This isn't as easy as I thought." Ron was now sharing the bottle of Merlot with Judy and frankly hoping that it led him to an evening of forgetting about the work that he had to do. "Have you developed the budget that Tom wants?" Judy asked. "Pretty much. I know what he wants. I have laid out numbers and I have developed a cash flow forecast. I'm starting to look at receivables procedures. I don't know how people who don't know numbers as well as I do it. One thing that is becoming obvious, even in something like receivables it is the system that is important. If I have a sound system and teach people to use it the results will come." "I like the wine?" "Me too." "What I am starting to understand is that I determine the amount of money that I make and that both my sales plan and what I expect from my employees is determined by my financial plan." "I think it's time for bed." "Me too."

Profit Controls

Tom's emails seemed more frequent now.

"Profit controls relate to the control of direct costs. Expense controls relate to the control of overhead. The most important key profit indicator (KPI) profit control is labor, which is a function of your organizational structure; however you need to develop some preliminary reporting controls to assist you. Job costing is the cornerstone of the company. You must know at all times if the jobs are on track to produce the targeted gross profit. The doctrine of true costs must be utilized. There must be knowledge of what it really costs to produce income. You write the checks but the employees spend the money. There must be a constant focus on the relationship between pricing and actual cost. Job costing is also central to any incentive

program. What you need to do is determine the results that you are expecting out of each position."

Tom

MANAGERIAL BUDGETING

DESIRED PROFIT

_____% (A)

PROFIT PLAN   _____% (A/2)

    NEW ASSET $_____
    DEBT PRINCIPAL $_____
    TAXES $_____
    CASH RETENTION $_____

TOTAL REQUIRED: $_____ (B)

SALES REQUIRED (B*2)/A
$_____
BREAK EVEN

COST OF GOODS SOLD:
_____% (C)
    (LABOR/MATERIALS AND
    OTHER DIRECT COSTS)

GROSS PROFIT:
_____% (100-C)

AVAIABLE FOR OVERHEAD
_____% (C-A)

DISTRIBUTION TO OWNER
_____% (A/2)

HIGHLIGHT 9

Ron realized that his direct costs consisted of labor, materials and some other costs that he wouldn't have if he didn't do the job. They were sort of the things that he could directly bill a customer for. In order to have profit controls he had to address the two major categories of labor and materials. Thinking that the material costs would be easier he found another accounting book and read the section regarding material costs.

"There are numerous factors that determine the company's material costs.[19] They include:

(1) Price negotiation;

(2) term negotiation;

(3) utilization of discounts offered;

(4) systems for assuring that company receives what was ordered at the price that was negotiated;

(5) assuring credit for damaged goods or short deliveries;

(6) controls that we are paying the negotiated price--once;

(7) establishing appropriate inventory levels and maintaining such;

(8) controlling obsolescence in inventory and damage in storage;

(9) controlling theft;

(10) freight negotiation;

(11) maintaining adequate inventory to assure ability to fill orders;

(12) terms charged;

(13) same day billing;

(14) And collections."

Ouch—so much for easy.

Equipment and Inventory

From his reading Ron also realized that equipment utilization controls also relate to direct costs. The company has fixed assets that he has to pay for whether he is using them or not. They make money when it is running; they lose money when it isn't.[20] **How will we determine if we should repair or sell? Buy or lease? In an equipment intense business or a business with a shop, the implementation of equipment strategies is critical. Ron outlined a preventive maintenance plan as it dawned on him, "My sales plan should coordinate with the utilization of equipment..." The cat just ignored this revelation. All sales are not equal. Sales that utilize under-utilized equipment are more valuable. Sales incentives should focus on equipment utilization."**

Inventory was an entire different issue. Ron listed inventory issues that he must address:

- Inventory Optimization. Identify the actual status of the current inventory—what do we have? What is obsolete? What is damaged? What should be kept? What should be disposed of?

- What is the actual value of the inventory?

- What is the book value of the inventory?

- What strategies should be used to reconcile these values with minimum tax obligation?

- How could the inventory be better controlled so that: (1) We know what we have; (2) the organization knows what we have; and (3) theft and obsolescence is minimized.

- What is the appropriate level of inventory?

- Who is and who should be responsible for the level of inventory?

- Will the results be measured in turns, dollars or otherwise?
- What strategies should be implemented to focus the company on the more profitable use of inventory?
- How will we measure those results?

"This looks like a good project for next year."

Ron also was confused by the fact that inventory and equipment were listed on his balance sheet instead of on his income statement. Controlling inventory and equipment utilization would directly effect his operating results so why weren't they on the income statement? "Have to talk to Patrick about that one."

Another email had arrived from Tom.

"After a company has identified the needs of their customers they then set goals intended to meet those needs. They then measure many things but often they fail to measure the very standard of "quality" that they purport to achieve. If your company is promising prompt delivery, are you measuring that result? "(E)mployees at all levels must understand exactly what the target is and how best to achieve it....these employees must have an accurate feedback system for determining whether the decisions they are making are, in fact, the ones that will accomplish the company's overall goals....The necessity of measuring results is particularly crucial for those employees who affect customer service through their work but who don't have face-to-face contact with those customers....they need clear targets and other means of measuring how well they are meeting their goals."[21]

Tom

"I think that I have a pretty good handle on my first two responsibilities." Ron and Judy had turned the bottle of wine into a daily ritual. Tonight it was a Washington Chardonnay—

and there was a second one in the refrigerator. "I must cause the business to earn a minimum mandatory percentage of profit. That profit must be enough to give us what we want personally. The only reason for this business to exist is to make our lives better." "I thought it was the chardonnay that made out life better!" "Might be Honey but we need the profit to buy it! I have to create cost controls to assure that the minimum mandatory percentage of profit is achieved. It has been a lot of work but I am glad that I have done it. Tomorrow I will start of my third responsibility—the people. It is the labor KPI that seems the greatest single factor..." Judy's lips on his caused him to stop. "Guess she liked the wine."

Saturday morning started later than normal. Ron was scrambling eggs waiting for Judy to rouse. By the time she came in her plate was ready. "Good morning. It's time to get to work!" Judy hesitated, contemplating loopholes in her promise to help. Finding none she poured a cup of coffee, thanked Ron for breakfast and bought a few minutes to eat. The coffee had it's desired effect and she pulled out her legal pad as she cleared her plate from the table. "Okay—get to it" she chimed.

"This was a good week. Tom used the term "tax accounting done backwards" and now I know what he means. I have developed a budget for the business based upon the minimum mandatory percentage of profit that the business requires. I have identified KPI's and am working on systems to monitor them. I am still working on dividing my business into profit centers and then using overhead allocation strategies to determine pricing but I want to do more of that when I start working on sales. I understand the difference between cash and profit and the need for both." Judy was busy writing.

Ron leaned back on his chair and thought some more trying to come up with something witty—suddenly the cat jumped on the table startling Ron almost causing him to fall backwards. Judy's laughing stopped saved the cat's last life. Ron stood with coffee poured all over his shirt and jeans. "Very funny."

"I'm sorry, it's the picture of you as a big-time business owner with coffee spilled all over you!" "Okay, okay." "Anything else for our notes—I'll leave out the part about the cat."

"Yes there is. We also reviewed equipment and inventory controls. Most of it doesn't apply yet." "Guess you have to have inventory and equipment before you have to control it." Judy was smiling and Ron had lightened up. "Guess so." "So what is on the clipboard of fun today?" Ron asked. "Just the grocery store—want to come with me?" "You know Judy, I'd love to but I think I better work on my inventory and equipment control." "Yeah right. Here are my notes. See you this afternoon and thanks for breakfast."

Judy left and Ron took shower and a nap.

Chapter Three – Passing Out The Hats

*Ron is responsible for taking his **people** and creating an organizational structure. The organizational structure focuses the company upon the enforcement of his cost controls and results in the production of his minimum mandatory percentage of profit.*

Chapter Outline

1. The "operating system"
2. Quantitative Analysis of Functionality
   a. Gaps
   b. Duplication
3. Incentives and Accountability
4. Entitlement and Fear
5. Delegation
6. Meetings and Communication

"It is nice to have goals, but the goal without a plan is only a wish." Ron was again reviewing the goal sheet from his father. "Having the goals is nice but I also need to have systems; procedures and controls designed to deliver the planned results." "Well your organizational structure is the delivery system of your plan. How are you going to do it?" Grace was challenging him again. Then she dropped the real bombshell, "All this work you are doing? Start putting it into a binder. What you are developing is your company's operating system.[22] Your computer has an operating system and so does your business. You will find this especially important because now you are starting to ask questions about handling employees. Remember the Operations Manual at Acme?" Things were coming into focus again for Ron. "Makes sense to me" he commented as Grace moved on to take care of her customers.

Ron knows that he is up for the task. He has developed his plan. He has determined what he wants. Now he is determining how to structure his people in order to deliver those results. What result does each person have to provide in order for the plan to be achieved? "*The company's Organizational Structure is the delivery system for Ron's pre-determined results—Grace is right.*" Once every job is examined in the context of Ron's plan, the results can be defined, however until I had developed the financial plan (budget) it was impossible to write a job description. When properly done, each person will understand the results that they must produce and the sum of those results will equate to my budget. They will understand that the company provides them with a paycheck in exchange for those results. The results will be constantly measured for the employee and for Ron. For Ron they will provide a comfort level in the knowledge that the results are being produced and for the employee they create a focus. **An employee's job is to deliver to Ron their pre-defined result. That result is derived from Ron's plan. They receive their paycheck for delivering those results; are held accountable for those results and are provided incentives to exceed those results. If each employee provides their results, the company achieves their results and the budget is met.**

Ron sat at the counter and watched as Grace left to serve the far table. "Is this too harsh? It seems like I'm being too tough on my employees. I want this to be a nice place to work." Grace worked her way back and he voiced his concerns to her.

"Ron, there are a few things that you will have to get over. First, you owe your employees two things—respect and opportunity. We have a duty to treat them with respect. We provide them good working conditions and treat them fairly and honestly. And we owe them an opportunity. If you do this right, you will have created a significant opportunity for each of your employees to be part of something they can be proud of and be able to obtain a level of income within the range of their chosen job that they can control. They will be proud of what they do and proud to work for you but you have to face the fact that not everyone will seize that opportunity. Some of them will only take part of it. At some point there is nothing else that you can do. Every company needs campers and you will have some. Don't feel badly about it."

"The second thing to be aware of is that you will not be able to be friends with your employees. You are different from them and they want you to be different from them. It is like the parent-child relationship. Remember when you were 16? You didn't want your parents out on a date with you, did you? Respect them, provide them opportunity and do your job of running the company. That is what they want."

He had another sip of coffee and was ready to leave when he saw Tom walk in the door. "Thought I could catch you here" Tom called out as he hung his coat on the wobbly coat rack by the door. "We need to talk some more."

Ron didn't know what to say. He was already overwhelmed with what Grace had said but he hadn't seen Tom since that first night. He looked much tanner. Expecting small talk Ron was taken aback when Tom continued on as if he knew exactly what Ron had been thinking.

"McDonalds has a cadre of MBA's constantly identifying a better, more "idiot-proof" system of delivering a consistently prepared hamburger—better than Grace's—with the lowest possible level of employee. Compare their effort in developing and refining their systems and procedures to the time and effort that you spend in developing you systems and procedures and is it any wonder that they have better systems than you do? You cannot manage people you can only manage systems. People do what <u>they</u> want to do; systems do what <u>you</u> want them to do."

"Imagine that you were going to set up the business in a city 1000 miles away. You are going to run the business from your home without ever going there. What would the jobs be? What result would each person have to achieve? How would they communicate with you each day so that you knew that they were really doing their jobs? Draw the organizational chart for that business identifying the functions rather than the people. That is the same structure that you should have at home. What is each position responsible for? Have all of the business' tasks been assigned? How can we measure the results of each job? How can it be simply communicated so the employees really understand it? How should they report their results to me? <u>Most importantly, how should they be held accountable for those results and what incentives can be provided for them to produce results *beyond* those that I am already paying them for?</u>"

Grace had placed a full coffee cup in front of Tom. Her actions made it clear to Ron that she knew Tom better than she had let on. She sat down to listen to Ron without saying a word. "People are going to do what they want to do. You must establish systems that make them want to do what <u>you</u> want done. First you must communicate to them what you want done and it must be done in a measurable form.[23] They must understand that those results are what they get paid to produce. One of their "results" that they must provide is timely reporting to you. This provides you with a comfort level in the knowledge that they have actually done their job. They must also understand that something bad is going to happen to them if they do not deliver their pre-determined result—accountability. Incentives are additional compensation for producing more profit for the company than they have already been paid to produce. Since profit is only generated by lowering expenses or increasing sales, the only cash incentives that a company can have are for efforts that either lower expenses or increase sales in an amount greater than they have already been paid to produce."

Quantitative analysis of functionality

"You're going to show him the quantitative analysis of functionality, aren't you?" mused Grace. "I think I'll go back to

Minding My Own Business

work." Tom continued undeterred. "In a quantitative analysis of functionality, each function of the business is defined in terms of the result that it must produce. As an organization that does not complete this work grows, it is will be apparent that positions were developed around people, not functions. The organization must be re-examined in terms of functions. Positions must be created and defined in terms of what the "system" requires of each position not in terms of what each employee wants to do. The proper assignment of all functions will eliminate <u>gaps and duplication.</u> Gaps are those functions that no one in the organization presently chooses to perform. Presently these unassigned functions all fall to Ron and interfere with his ability to do his job. Duplication is when more than one person chooses to perform the same function. This is the root of "finger pointing" and is often done be employees referred to as "empire builders." It is critical to remember that you own the business, you own the system and you, and not your employees determine which positions perform which functions. In a small business people often wear more than one hat—which is fine—what cannot happen is *more than one person cannot wear the same hat.* A company, which does not regularly perform this task, ends up in organizational chaos. Duplication and gaps are the leading cause of inefficiency."

When you own a business what you actually "own" is a system. It is a system that converts <u>market demand for your product or service</u> into <u>cash in the bank</u>. All of the tasks that have to take place to convert that market demand into cash have to be identified and then assigned (in a position guide or job description) to the proper position. When a person fills a position, they are responsible for each task assigned to that position—responsible for the results that are required of each task.

Work on your system—it is all that you really own. The neglect of their system is the most common cause of inefficiency and lost profit in a company.

HIGHLIGHT 10

"What are you doing here anyway?" Ron finally had to ask. Tom just ignored him and continued on. "Each function is then defined in terms of a result. It is not sufficient to merely state the tasks that you expect of each person. You must convey to them the result that you expect. Job descriptions must be written in terms of measurable results, not as a list of tasks. The results for each function are determined by the results that are needed to accomplish your financial plan.[24] When you have each position's functions defined in terms of a measurable result you can establish accountability. You cannot have accountability without it."

"Incentives now can become rational—they are bonuses paid for performance exceeding the result that you have paid them for. Cash bonuses can only be paid for results that either increase sales above the plan or reduce costs below the plan."

Tom finally turned his attention to the coffee but at this point Ron was so enthralled that he didn't even care why Tom had walked in. There was a long pause. Ron was allowing what Tom had said to sink in and Tom was catching his breath. Grace rejoined them and put a piece of pie in front of them both. As Ron was beginning to see the benefits of putting his "system" on paper Tom interrupted his thoughts.

"**This is often the most important organizational exercise that a company can perform.** This analysis provides a rational basis for compensation, accountability and incentives—organizational structure. This company is currently no where near able to establish systems of compensation, accountability and incentives upon a rational basis."

"Each job description is written in terms of a measurable result. The employee then becomes responsible for performing that result. The result must be the focus of the employee's day. That focus is communicated through daily or weekly reporting that in a simple manner identifies whether or not the employee has accomplished their short-term result. If they have not accomplished their short term result they are immediately held accountable with an immediate management meeting where they are asked two questions—why didn't they accomplish their result and what are they going to do to immediately change it? "

"Formal reviews must be held 2-4 times per year and are tied to criteria for pay raises. These reviews are critical—failure to hold them on their regular basis creates a serious morale issue."

Ron finally had to ask, "Do people really do this stuff?" Ron was embarrassed with his comment because he remembered so much of what Tom had laid out from Acme. Tom and Ross O'Donoghue would get along famously! Grace walked to the back room and returned with pages in her hand. "These define each task we do here and the results that are expected from it. Any other questions?" Running a diner can be just cooking and cleaning; making money is planning, monitoring, and planning some more. It doesn't just "happen" you have to make it happen.

Incentives and Accountability

Tom had finished his pie. Putting his fork down on the empty plate he went on. "Virtually no small businesses have a rational incentive plan. The successful businesses like Grace's have completed the groundwork. If you don't know what results a person is expected to provide in exchange for their paycheck, how can you pay them an incentive for exceeding them?

Businesses have 3 groups of employees—climbers, campers and quitters. The percentages vary but basically the top 15-25% are the employees who are making the company money (climbers). This small group of people earn a company close to 80% of their money. The next 60-70% are just sort of there neither helping nor hurting the bottom line (campers). Although this is by far the biggest group, they only make the company about 30% of their money. You can't have a company of all climbers—all-star teams don't win games. The campers are required so that you can do the volume of work that you require. The ones that you can do away with are your quitters. These are the last 5-15% of the people and they often cost the company about 10% of their money.

Owners often tell me that they want all of their employees to be happy. Why? There is no reason to want everyone "happy." You want the climbers wildly happy and the quitters uncomfortable. Yet most companies under-compensate the climbers in order to subsidize the quitters. So now who is the most likely to go pursue other job offers? You end up with turnover in the wrong group. In fact you want to over-compensate your climbers at the cost of the quitters so that those bottom people change or leave. Beware of the organization where entitlement has become a way of life. "I get a raise because I've been here, not because I produce more." "I get a promotion because I have the most seniority." "I get a bonus because it is December 25th, not because of what I did." Entitlement is a disassociation of compensation from results. Many profit sharing and bonus plans encourage entitlement and are actually destructive to the company. It causes turnover in the wrong group of people. *Remember that people need to know what results are expected in exchange for their paycheck and what results beyond that will produce additional compensation."*

Ron's mind drifted off to Acme. One of his major complaints had been when he was held accountable for results that he couldn't control. He recalled when they scrapped their incentive plan—the one that gave everyone a year-end bonus—and replaced it with their merit review. Oh did some people complain—but they were the weak ones. Ron kind of liked it.

"Remember also that you cannot hold a person accountable for a result that they cannot control." Tom hadn't missed a beat. "You must provide people with the authority to control the outcome of anything that you are going to hold them accountable for.[25] However the defined results must kept simple. If they are too complicated they become ineffective. They must be appropriate for the person performing the task. An unreasonably complicated formula to define results may be permissible for a high-level employee but clearly is unacceptable for positions held by less-educated people. Keep it simple."

"Before I go on, it's time to answer your question, "Why am I here?" I could tell from your development of the budget that you were really starting to catch on. The people part of the business is so important and I knew that you were ready." Tom took another sip of coffee. "I left my cruise early and came back to talk with you in person about this. I learned from the best. He would do anything for anyone who really wanted to learn how to run a business and I guess that I am just repaying that debt." Ron didn't have a response. "Thanks" was all that came out. "Let's keep going. You are handling this well and a lot of it is because you understand how the numbers affect the company and the people. You can manage numbers and the numbers can manage people."

"Organizational structure cannot work without measurement. Subjective standards are no standards. Objective and clear standards must be established and enforced consistently. Owners are often reluctant to do so and in their effort to "be nice" and "keep people happy" they are actually shooting themselves in the foot. Loyalty is a one-way street. Very few of your employees will be here in 10 years but you will be."

Ron thought back to Acme where indeed by the time he was there ten years he was one of the senior people.

"Your loyalty must be to <u>your system</u> and people will grow and benefit from this focus. You make money and you are doing your greatest service to your employees. You are not going to make everyone happy anyway so take care of the people who produce your money. The others are whiners."

"The use of incentives is critical in addressing the "what's in it for me" mentality of the modern work force. We have to have incentives or we cannot have accountability—but we cannot pay a bonus for a result that we have already paid for in their wage. People who produce profits for the company beyond that which you have already paid them to produce should be allowed to share in that additional profit that they have produced. This is the basis of excess-based profit incentives. It is critical that the incentive relate back to the basic budget of the business."

"So, as I see it, in order to effectively manage[26] I have to do five things." Ron started writing on the back of the napkin as he spoke. He made the following list:

1. Employees must understand what results are expected of them;

2. Employees must understand how those results are measured;

3. Employees must know if their results have met the minimum level of expected performance;

4. The frequency that employees must report those results and be held accountable must be determined by their level of authority;

5. There must be immediate feedback for unacceptable results with a meeting where the manager asks two questions—"Why did we fail? And what are we going to change tomorrow?"

"Bingo!" Tom was pleased. "Ever heard of micro-management? Everyone knows that micro-management is wrong but few people really know what they are talking about when they use this term. Micro-management takes place when the supervisor (owner) is more concerned with the process than with the result. Manage results, don't manage process. This is a critical distinction. Employees resist being held accountable for the "way" that they do something but understand being held accountable for a result that they did not accomplish. When the emphasis is shifted to the result, then the manager can use a failing result as an opportunity to train the desired process. If the manager merely harps upon the process insisting that it be done the way he or she did it then they will fail in their corrective action."

"I need a break," Tom stated as he rose from his chair. "I've had too much coffee!" His fork dropped to the floor as he stood gaining the attention again of Grace who had just finished serving a customer at the counter. As Tom made his way to the rest room, Grace came by to refill their cups. "Tom is good isn't he? We have known each other for years. We both went into business about the same time and owe a huge debt to a guy who took us under his wing. Our agreement was that we would help other people as he did us. Tom has been a lot more diligent with it, but then he grew his business, sold it and has the time. I just like the diner and plan to be here forever." Tom was returning and looking ready to go back at it.

"So talk about how productivity, entitlement and fear relate to each."

Tom smiled at Grace. "There is a book, "<u>Danger in the Comfort Zone</u>" by Judith Bardwick.[27] In it she describes a continuum from Entitlement on one side and Fear on the other. Her theory is that you get your maximum productivity from employees when you are in the middle and not strongly in either mode. Entitlement is a "disassociation between compensation and results." Your employees fail to associate the result that they provide with the compensation that they receive. They don't understand (and possible you don't either) why they get a paycheck each week. Basically they feel like you "owe them" and they are "entitled. Obviously in this mode you will not have highly productive employees."

"In a Fear Mode, employees are scared, cynical, resentful, apathetic, and mistrustful. A company cannot produce its greatest earnings in this environment. There is a lack of understanding of where the company is going and how employees fit into that picture. This symptom is usually a communication issue."

"It is important to understand your employees because the remedial actions that you have to take to move them from entitlement are exactly the opposite actions that you need to take to move them from fear.[28] You still with me?" Ron seemed to be somewhat lost. "So I can't always take the same actions to increase productivity?" "Afraid not." Ron nodded and made some more notes on the pad that he now carried constantly.

Grace had left the table to wait on other customers. She returned as Ron was writing. "What was amazing to me" Grace chimed in as if she had never left the table "was learning the significant impact of even minor increases in productivity." She was giving Tom another opening.

"Right." Tom took his cue. "Of course you have to be able to measure something to improve it. You need to be able to answer questions like, "What is your labor margin for this week's schedule of production? What does your labor margin have to be in order to meeting your profit objective? How do you measure it? Who is responsible for your labor margin? How do you communicate the standards to your people?" Without answers to these questions it is impossible to control labor costs. A mere three minutes of additional work per hour through better control of labor, would produce 24 additional work minutes—*a 5.5% increase in productivity!*"[29]

"Is 5.5% a lot?" "Well figure out 5% of your annual payroll and you tell me." Ron let this sink in. "Managing really is critical isn't it? Obviously I cannot spend all of my time managing people because I have my own job so what, I have to delegate?"

"Delegation is a learned technique. In order to effectively delegate a task there are a number of steps that must be taken. Stephen Covey refers to the delegation process as, "Creating Win-Win Stewardship Agreements"[30] First the task must be clearly defined—specify the desired results." Tom had not lost his stride. "It is vital that the desired results are *results, not methods.* Often times the task looks different in the eyes of the two parties. In order to accomplish a meeting of the minds you must define the task in terms of results. The result is what is critical and is what must be clearly defined. The definition must include measurement—how will it be determined if the results have been achieved? The person must not only understand what result is required, they must also understand and agree as to how the result is being measured. Once the desired result is agreed upon, the parties then agree upon how the result should be achieved—the steps that must be taken and *guidelines* must be set. Within those guidelines is the level of authority that the person has. There are six levels of authority—(1) wait until told; (2) ask; (3) Recommend; (4) Act and report immediately; (5) Act and report periodically; and (6) Act on own.[31] This defines the level of authority that has been delegated. These levels change as you gain or lose trust in the person."

"The third, fourth and fifth steps identified by Covey are to identify the available resources (human, technical, financial, etc., define accountability (essential to the integrity of the delegation), and to determine the consequences—what happens if the result is or is not achieved both to the individual and the organization. Lastly, the parties must agree upon a feedback system. The person must be providing enough feedback to provide you with a comfort level of knowing that they are on track to achieve the result. The feedback can be formal (such as a report) or it may be informal (such as sticking his head in your office twice a day to let you know where he stands) but regardless it must be complied with. It is the feedback element that is most commonly ignored."

"Effective delegation relieves your obligations and develops employees. "A leader is not appointed because he knows everything and can make every decision. He is appointed to bring together the knowledge that is available and then create the prerequisites for the work to be done. He creates the systems that enable him to delegate responsibility for day-to-day operations."[32]

"I could delegate if I had competent middle management…" the words were not even out of Ron's mouth before he regretted saying them. Tom was ready.

"Some companies have only the owner and its workers. There are few other employees responsible enough to take on management roles. This is a critical issue in succession of the business and in reducing the time obligations of the owner." Ron recognized that one of the reasons why Acme hardly missed him is that it seemed like they were always training someone for the next job. They developed people for positions.

"Management personnel don't just arrive—they have to be developed. The management style of some owners has inhibited the development of people. There probably have been some people in the past that were of management level competency left the company. Opportunities for development of employees must be encouraged. An owner with a reputation as a "control" person will not accumulate good people around him. The other side of the coin is that the people you need may very well already be here, they simply need to be given the opportunity. Controls allow people to be given that opportunity with also being given the ability to sink the ship."

Minding My Own Business

"I have to talk to them? I thought hiring and paying them was enough" Ron joked. Even Tom smiled at this.

"Communications are vital in any business. Employees often complain about communications without really even knowing what they mean. There are numerous ways that a company communicates with its people—written memos, meetings, e-mails, informal meetings, phone calls and messages—but what is important first is <u>what</u> is communicated, not how."

"An employee needs to have information sufficient for them to do their job. *In order to do their job they must have a basic understanding of the company's direction, the company's structure, what is expected of them and whether or not their performance is producing what is expected. Ideally they will also know what they can do to increase their compensation and the measures of those results.*"

Ron caught Grace's eye and held up his coffee cup. "I guess then the logical next issue is how we communicate to employees—what do we have to do to get them this information. Should I have meetings, memos or what?"

Tom smiled, "you used the right word. Communicating is what you have to do and it has to be done in all of those ways. There is a time and place for each." "But people hate meetings—so do I! That's part of what drove me crazy at Acme."

"Meetings can be lengthy and costly. The hourly cost of a meeting of key personnel can run into the thousands of dollars and therefore the methods of communicating must be examined. Meetings are still required, but effective meetings that communicate in a minimum amount of time are essential. As we will talk about later, the real reason form meetings is sales." Ron gave Tom a puzzle look. "People have to meet face-to-face on some sort of a regular basis. An owner who holds "informal meetings" with each of his people individually each day runs the risk of people suspecting that he is saying one thing to some people and another thing to them. Such policy breeds distrust."

"Lay out a meeting schedule. You have to have some meetings for long-term issues—say once a quarter or once a year. Maybe tie them to a company function. This is to communicate the company's long-term direction and focus. Then you need an intermediate meeting—monthly of all key players to monitor results of some long-term issues. Also there are weekly meetings to monitor results and daily huddles."

"How will work ever get done if we have all these meetings?" "Done right, it's not a problem—done wrong it is."

"Time for a break. Let's order some dinner." Grace brought out their order. It turns out that Tom would only be in town for a day or two and then was leaving again. "Do you know Grace?" Ron asked. "We both had the same teacher" was all Tom said.

Grace had set a chicken fried steak in front of Tom and it seemed that even the smell of food was enough to send him back into his lecturing mode. "Ron, you are a football fan. A football team will have a game plan, practice the game plan all week but during the game before every play they still have a huddle. Companies are the same. There needs to be a communication of the vision or game plan. There needs to be weekly focus in management meetings regarding the current part of the game plan and <u>every day</u> there needs to be a huddle. Five-minute huddles should take place in management and in each department. They are mandatory with no tolerance for non-attendance and no tolerance for them lasting more than five-minutes."

"Almost regardless of the economy, everyone who you would want to hire is working. You can no longer take the same approach to staffing that you could in a slow economy. Your next employees are currently working for someone else—and your employees are looked at as someone else's next employees."

"Turnover is one of the most expensive events in a company. When turnover occurs the costs include: the lost production when the person leaves, the cost of outplacement, the risk of legal claims by the departing employee, the cost of the time spent placing ads and interviewing, the cost of the lost productivity during the new employees first weeks, and the cost of the lost productivity from the person training the new person. Turnover is inevitable, but we want to be sure that turnover occurs in our quitters and not in our climbers. Companies with high turnover rates generally lack in at least one of the following three areas."

"Recruitment—the company needs to convey during the recruitment process the company's mission. The incoming employee needs to understand what the corporate culture is in the business and be "sold" on being a part of that team.[33] We cannot merely recruit the unemployed. The fact is we are going to be taking someone else's employees—and they are going to be trying to take ours. The recruitment process must be designed to address this issue and get quality employees who are going to stick with the company."

Four Elements of a Staffing Plan:

- Recruitment
- Training
- Development
- Retention

HIGHLIGHT 11

"Development--a company must offer their people the opportunity to "move up." This is why growth in a company is required. *You may not want to grow, but if you don't you will die. Failure to grow eliminates the development opportunities of you best employees and causes them to leave for better opportunities.* Not all employees want to develop, but your best ones do. Therefore it is crucial that the opportunities within a company be identified and communicated to each employee."

"Retention--what keeps your employees working here if someone across the street offers them $1 per hour more? This is where benefits, working conditions, and morale come into play. It can even be argued that development opportunities are really retention devices. There needs to be a plan for retention or you end up with turnover."

"Training is 25% technical and 75% teaching of the company's system. You don't hire someone unless they have some basic ability to do the job but you do hire people who really don't know how your system works. It is critical that a new employee has something that explains to them—this is what your job is and this is how you do it."

"Systems and structure work. People live in chaos. Their personal lives are a mess. We want to provide for them a place where there is a predictable system. Where they know what is expected of them and where for 8 hours a day they have structure. Young children will play the same videotape over and over again to fill the psychological need for predictability. When tied to a system of development or promotion for employees you significantly reduce turnover. **But you must be willing to constantly work on your system and you must be disciplined enough to consistently enforce it. If you cannot respect your system then you cannot expect your employees to respect it.**"

"*In order to have an effective "system" of operations it must be documented.* Each function must be documented so that consistency is achieved. The importance of the documentation becomes evident when there is turnover. The new person must have something that they can pick up and say, "This is how I do my job." This is critical if the business is going to become systems dependent rather than people dependent. Every football team has a playbook."

"*The Operations Manual describes how the company would work if it was 1000 miles away and you could never visit. It describes how each job is done and what each person has to do so that their boss has a comfort level of knowing that the job has been done. Remember that it is a constant work-in-progress."*[34]

"There is a constant competing struggle between the need for documentation and the need to reduce paperwork. The paperwork that is used must have a minimum number of "touches" and must not duplicate other paperwork. Effective computerization often solves much of this problem, however the problem of <u>information flow</u> can continue even after the problem of paper flow is solved."

"I obviously have a lot more work to do." Ron felt challenged but not overwhelmed. "Why do I need to do it before I open—why can't I just develop it later? Then I could get some quicker revenue?" "Wishful thinking Ron. If you were going to start a kennel, would you first bring in the dogs or would your first build the cages?" "You're right of course. I will email you the organizational structure when I finish it up." "Great. We can stay in touch. I'll be here a few days."

Ron was tired, "Do I really have to write it all down?" Tom was ready, "God wrote it down for Moses—and in stone no less! Why did he do that? Well if he didn't imagine what the Ten Commandments would be like now! Thou shall not kill—unless I don't like the person…Thou shall not commit adultery except on weekends….You get the gist."

"Before you get too far into it I want you to talk with Brent. Brent is an HR person I know who really understands the relationship between recruitment, development, training and retention." Tom wrote a phone number on his napkin and told Ron to use his name when he called. The chicken fried steak was cold by now but that didn't stop Tom—and when he finished he asked for seconds.

Brent's office turned out to be a comfortable setting. Ron sat back in a deep chair and observing the open can on Brent's desk he accepted the offer of Diet Pepsi. "I suspect that Tom wanted me to tell you our hiring process?" Ron just gave him a look that said, "he didn't say but it sounds interesting."

"Whenever someone is hired here we always do the same thing. I screen the person and then the people who they will work with have input. If it is someone that we will offer a position to then Mr. White, our owner gets involved. We have an applicant coming in shortly. I will ask if we can sit in." Brent picked up the phone and moments later we were escorted into Mr. White's office where a young lady sat dressed for an interview with her prospective boss. Mr. White nodded to us and we sat down in chairs on the other side of the room from where Katy, the applicant sat facing Mr. White. Mr. White didn't hesitate—you got the impression that this wasn't his first barbeque.

"Katy I have your resume here and you look qualified. Certainly if Brent feels you can do the job you can. We completely support Brent's decisions in hiring; however I am not going to hire you today." The pregnant pause brought a disappointed look to Katy's face. Mr. White went on, "before we can hire you I have to make sure that you understand the conditions that we have on our employment and that you really are committed to working within these conditions. We have three basic conditions of working here and if you violate any of these conditions, you will be fired on the spot. Since it is expensive and not good for either you or our company to have turnover, we need you to understand these conditions and then to discuss them with your friends and family before deciding to accept our position. I am going to explain these conditions and then you go home and think about it. Fair enough?" Katy nodded.

"The first condition of working here is to have a positive attitude. We are a small business and we have to deal with the public and each other. Sometimes it is difficult and we have found that negative attitudes are a real deterrent to accomplishing our mission. We demand that at all times while on our premises that you exhibit a positive attitude. If one day

Minding My Own Business

you get up and decide that you cannot have a positive attitude on that day, call Brent or your supervisor and don't come in. We cannot have anything but positive attitudes here. If at anytime you do not exhibit a positive attitude, we have to fire you on the spot. Can you live with this condition, Katy?" Katy said she could.

"The second condition is that since we are small you are going to have to ask others for help and they will be asking you. We are a team and you are expected to act like you are a part of that team. We expect teamwork. If at anytime you cannot act as part of our team, we have to fire you on the spot. Can you live with this condition, Katy?" Again Katy said that she could and she seemed more confident in her answer this time.

"Lastly, there is a third condition of working here." Katy leaned forward to hear this one. "We know that you used to work at Pacific and we respect what they do. As you progress we expect that you will find things that you would like to change and will want to make suggestions. My door is always open. I want to hear how we can make things better. I will listen to you and then we will decide if we want to adopt the changes that you suggest however in the meantime we have a system. We have worked very hard on our system and we will continue to adopt changes to our system—but until we change our system, everyone is expected <u>to use</u> our system. If people do not use the same system you end up with chaos. Until we change our system you will use our system and if at any time you are not using our system we will have to fire you on the spot." Katy interrupted, "but how will I know the system?" "You will be given training. We will teach you how we do things here. We are good at that. If you don't know, ask. Once you have been taught the system, you must use it." "That sounds fair."

"So Katy, go home tonight and talk about these conditions—Brent will give you the written copy in your job description—and talk it over. If you want to be a part of our team, come back at 9 tomorrow morning and report to Brent. If you cannot live with these conditions, please do us all a favor and don't come back tomorrow. We'd like to have you—you seem very capable."

Katy, Brent and Mr. White completed their formalities and I was left alone with Mr. White. We introduced ourselves and I complimented him on his hiring technique. "Glad you had a chance to see it. We have found that this has completely changed the attitude of our employees and makes firing when we have to much easier." "I can see that." Ron was trying to sound intelligent. It was time to get home—Judy was cooking a roast and she had said that she wanted to eat early which was always a good sign. "Thank you so much." Mr. White smiled and returned the compliment. Somehow it seemed that he knew something that Ron didn't.

The roast and pinot noir had it's desired effect. Ron didn't get around to writing that night but when Judy left for work the next morning he spent the entire day putting together his thoughts.

He started by documenting his system. He made a list of all of the functions that have to take place in order to convert market demand for his product into cash in his bank. From there he broke down each function into all of the tasks that were required.[35] He examined each task to determine what results would be required to produce his desired result and then sorted them into job descriptions. In doing this he identified potential gaps and duplication and was able to address these before they became problems.

When it was completed and bound in his operations manual it was amazing to see his system documented and organized for his control. It was also clear that by communicating the system to his employees, they would be in "alignment" with his desired results. Alignment is critical. The interests of the employee must match the interests of the company. This is accomplished through an effective system, coordinated with the company's financial plan and implemented through rational systems of accountability and incentives.

Done correctly the incentives are the owner's "steering wheel." They give the owner the ability to change the behavior of the employees to match a corporate objective. It is also obvious that an incentive program is at the top of a pyramid whose base is a well-conceived organizational structure.

Judy arrived home with her arms full. Ron took the groceries and gave her the legal pad. He spoke as he emptied the bags. "I really see the need to have an operating system for the business—probably always did but I never before knew what an operating system was. I put together a quantitative analysis of functionality so that I can eliminate gaps and duplication in my system. Can't say it was easy but it is really neat to see my "system" on paper." Judy was writing furiously.

"From the budget and this work it is easy to see how I can hold employees accountable and create meaningful incentives that are excess-profit based." Judy nodded. The system requires communication. I have developed an entire meeting system and the position descriptions alone help communicate to the employee the results that I require from each one. They also allow me to effectively delegate."

"Delegation and productivity are tough issues. I learned the levels of responsibility that can be delegated and the relationship between fear and entitlement in regards to the productivity of the labor force." Judy held up her hand. "Slow down!" "That was it" "Big week wasn't it!" "I accomplished a lot. We are definitely moving in the right direction." Judy ripped the pages off of her pad and handed them to Ron. "I'm moving in the right direction too—want to take a nap." Ron almost missed the wink.

Chapter Four – People Buy From People

Ron is responsible for selling both externally and internally.

Sales starts by defining why your customers should buy from you instead of your competition.

Chapter Outline

1. The USP
2. Lead Generation
3. Lead Qualification
4. Closing
5. Customer Service
6. Pricing and use of Break Even
7. Internal sellin

Ron had finished the organizational structure and emailed it to Tom. He now understood the first three of his responsibilities. He must produce a minimum mandatory percentage of profit. He had determined that amount and created a strategic plan. He had identified his long and short-term goals for himself and the business. He had created cost controls to assure that the minimum mandatory percentage of profit would actually be created. To do this he had created budgets and cash flows and other controls. Since meeting with Tom he had developed an organizational structure with incentives and accountability that would enforce the cost controls to assure that the minimum mandatory percentage of profit would be generated. Now it was time to look at sales.

> In Highlight 8 you determined your true break even. It is critical that you sales plan be designed to produce sales that meet or exceed this break even.
>
> **HIGHLIGHT 12**

Tom had already sent another email and beside the computer sat another letter from Ron's father. "The email comes first," Ron thought.

Real selling is selling value. Selling price is not really selling—lower the price enough and you are just giving your product away. Selling happens when you <u>raise</u> the price above market and have to convince your customer of the benefit of buying it anyway. Price selling causes the product to become a commodity. Commodities are interchangeable products upon which the customer buys based upon price alone. Commodities can be sold without a sales staff. Selling value is the only real function of a sales staff.

The first step in selling value is to differentiate your product in the mind of the buyer. You (and your buyer) should be able to answer the question, "Why should someone buy from me instead of my competitor?" This is your Unique Selling Proposal (USP). If your USP is not clearly defined then you have no chance. Remember that your USP must be defined from the perspective of the customer. There are certainly many reasons from your prospective as to why customers should buy from you instead of your competitor, but the only thing that matters is the perspective of the customer. The only relevant responses to be included in your USP are the reasons that are relevant to the customer's perspective. To understand what is relevant to your prospective customer you must first identify his pain. People run from pain much faster than they run to pleasure. What is your customer's pain? How do the benefits of your product address that pain? This is what you need to communicate to the prospective customer in order to convert them into a paying customer.

Therefore your USP is a statement of your product's benefits which addresses the pain of your prospective customers. This statement answers the question posed earlier.

A buyer <u>needs</u> to know that you can address his pain and he also <u>wants</u> to know that he can <u>trust</u> you to perform. Performance means doing what you said that you would do at a cost-to-benefit ratio that makes sense.

People buy from people. They must first trust the person selling. Commodity sales do not require the trust since the products are interchangeable and are sold only by price. Trust is the intangible that an effective salesperson must possess. Trust is a function of credibility and personality. Personality cannot be taught. An effective selling personality requires presence and instinct. You must seek out this personality in the persons that you hire. Hire personality and work ethic—the rest you can train. Credibility is obtained through preparation. Product knowledge, market knowledge, industry knowledge, client knowledge, professionalism and empathy are all factors in credibility. The first factors are obvious; empathy for the pain of the client needs additional explanation. The client needs to know that you have listened to him. Sales people must listen to be effective. The client generally believes that his circumstances are unique. He does not want sympathy from you, rather he wants empathy. Empathy is a validation of his pain with a plan to fix it. He gets excuses every day. He wants recognition of the issues that he faces tied to a solution. The greatest credibility comes from presenting a solution that is broader than your product.

An effective salesperson listens, repeats back the client's pain and proposes a solution that is broader than his product alone. Read the sales book and we will talk again.

Tom

"Okay so what has Dad sent, another article?" Ron opened the envelope and removed a single sheet of paper. "This could be a chain letter for as personal as this is" Ron mused aloud. The page had been removed from an older book and had no caption or heading.

"All salespersons claim to have a "quality" product however quality is different from the perspective of the seller and of the buyer. The only relevant perspective is that of the buyer. From the customer's prospective quality is a consistency of customer experience. The client needs to know what they can depend upon and then receive it. Quality is not having the best product—it is producing a consistent customer experience so that every time they buy they are getting the same result. Sales can be generated without a convergence of sales and production however this creates a customer service nightmare. Convergence is matching the way the product is sold with the way the company performs. Consistency of message, marketing, methods, treatment of the client, and levels of professionalism are required for a customer's perception of quality. This convergence generates repeat customers and negotiated work."

Judy sat reading in front of the fireplace, Ron joined her. He held the page from his father. "I wish Dad would be more help. Tom has been tremendous and Dad has no clue of what I am trying to do. Now he sends me some page he tore out of a book." "Ron, you are too hard on your Dad." He stuck the page in the back of the book that Tom had left him and started reading without commenting on Judy's reply.

The book was interesting. It reminded Ron a lot of the work that he had already done on his USP but it was saying things in a different way. "In order to have focus you must: (1) position yourself in your prospect's mind; (2) your position should be singular—one simple message; (3) your position must set you apart from your competitors; and (4) you must sacrifice—you cannot be all things to all people, you must focus on one thing.[36] You must create a positioning statement and sell it to your employees and your customers. To create a positioning statement, answer the following questions: Who: Who are you? What: What business are you in? For whom: What people do you serve? What need: What are the special needs of the people you serve? Against whom: With whom are you competing? What's different: What makes you different from those competitors? So: What's the benefit? What unique benefit does a client derive from your service?[37] If you cannot tell people why they should buy from you instead of from your competition, then how can you expect your customers to differentiate you from your competitors?

"All businesses are subject to basic, fundamental laws. The first basic, fundamental law is *that you are much more likely to achieve something if you first know what it is that you are trying to achieve.* The positioning statement is the "true north" of the company. In defining it, we define what it is that we are trying to achieve."

Tom had defined the difference between Sales and Marketing as follows: Marketing generates leads, Sales converts the leads to sales. Ron knew that both of these functions are required in any organization. Your company must generate leads. It could be for the purpose of generating relationships for negotiated work or it may be merely identifying bid opportunities. Once you have leads, you must convert them to sales. This can involve the estimating function, relationships, and numerous other functions.

The book, which was really a binder, went on. "An effective Sales and Marketing plan is an extension of the Strategic Plan. First you must identify your company's Unique Selling Proposal—why people should buy from you instead of your competitor." Ron immediately flashed back to the time that he had already invested in developing a USP with his goals and was thankful now that he had done so. "Then you must identify your targeted market and determine how you are going to get your message to them. The business requires a certain level of sales in order for the business to generate the results that you need.[38] Your sales management is then the accomplishment of that result."

The following day Ron had lunch scheduled with an old friend. The timing was perfect because Kyle was in sales management. She was making a lot of money so she probably knew what she was talking about. Ron drove to the other side of town—Kyle had chosen the restaurant. He arrived early and waited in the lobby for Kyle's appearance. Moments later Kyle greeted him enthusiastically—Kyle was always enthusiastic. They were seated and Kyle ordered a Rueben without looking at the menu. She made a face when the waitress suggested French fries and asked for a side salad. Meanwhile Ron was stumbling through the menu—it had been a while since he had eaten outside of the diner—and finally he ordered a club sandwich—with French fries. Kyle went straight to business. "The sales functions consist of lead generation, lead qualification, and closing. Let's look at each of these. Lead generation is simply generating the names of potential clients. A low level employee can be hired to generate a list of potential leads—or it could even be bought. One of the most effective ways to generate leads is to simply sit on the phone and call prospects. A low level employee can do it because you can just script the call and ask them to gather some basic information—it can even be outsourced."

"Lead qualification consists of taking the list of leads generated and determining which leads "qualify." You determine the parameters which qualify a lead. Again this can be done with a rather low level employee—or with spare time of an existing employee. Most companies make the mistake of hiring a high paid person who is capable of performing functions as well as closing to perform these rather low-level tasks. This results in a significant lack of productivity and creates a very undesirable situation. Being the only person to contact a potential client, this sales person has the ability to hold you hostage. It is much healthier to have the client bond to the company—or the sales process—than to a single individual."

The waitress brought out their water and ice tea. Kyle went on. "Lead generation is a low-paid position—it should not be performed by your high-priced person. Lead qualification is only slightly more involved. By qualifying I mean they meet criteria that you identify. A typical qualifying criteria might be "they use our product and plan to buy in the next six months." The person qualifying leads needs to be a slightly higher level person than the person doing lead generation. After you have qualified prospects, you must convert them to customers—close them. This is a task for your best sales people."

THE SALES PROCESS

GENERATE LEADS
QUALIFY LEADS
CLOSE
CUSTOMER SERVICE

HIGHLIGHT 13

"An effective sales structure takes your strong closers (who are highly paid) and puts them in front of as many qualified leads per day as possible. These people may or may not be your "relationship builders"—people who go out and "smooze" with customers (this is generally more of a customer service function) and they do not need to have extensive technical knowledge. They must know what they are talking about but they should be pushing technical questions back into the office and into the hands of the truly technical people—people who by their very nature are also lousy sales people! Relieving them of the burden of having to possess complete technical knowledge allows them to do what they do best. Remember this Ron—manage to people's abilities, not to their disabilities."

The arrival of lunch created a natural lull in the conversation. After adding hot mustard to her sandwich, Kyle went on. "With this type of sales structure, the customer bonds to the company rather than a sales person, this is a much "healthier" result. You never want to have anyone capable of holding you hostage. A mistake that many organizations make is hiring a "hot shot." It can be a strategy for a quick fix but it is never a long-term answer. You are much better off building a sales structure that produces the results. The sales structure can have interchangeable parts and not be "people dependent." If you do it right the system produces the revenue, not the people. When hiring a "hot shot" they come from someone else—just remember that they clients they bring will leave with them too. They also want to tell you how to run your business, they cost too much, they are hard to find, and they bring with them the mistakes of their past. Basically they are trouble. Hire attitude and work ethic. If your system is strong and you hire attitude and work ethic you will prevail in the long run."

Ron chewed on his club sandwich while soaking it all in. "So how does pricing come into play in a sales plan?" he asked. "Glad you asked" Kyle looked excited that she had a pupil.

Break even

"No Sales and Marketing plan can be effective without incorporating pricing schemes. The price of every job incorporates three components—the cost of doing the job, the job's contribution to profit and the job's contribution to overhead. It is critical to know your break even. Since the company's overhead is fixed, sales above the break even do not require a contribution to overhead. The farther you project sales above your break even, the more you can discount from your standard pricing. One simple way of computing break even is to take your fixed expenses and divide it by your gross profit. With effective sales projections and control of the break even, the company can know how much and how often it can "sharpen the pencil." Market penetration can be generated while maintaining pre-determined profit levels. Your sales plan must be designed to "win" the game. It cannot be left to chance. You will see some big boys coming in with low bids and you wonder how—they are using their break even discounts to target that job. In order to compete with the big boys you need big boy tools. Very few organizations have really developed these tools or have created a true sales structure. It is the sales structure that should be producing the sales, not the individual people."

> In Highlight 9 you projected your break even. If you plan to move sales above the break even you do not need to collect a contribution to overhead for the excess and therefore you can reduce your price by that much.
>
> (Projected Sales Volume − Break Even) x Overhead % = Discounts
>
> Discounts are the cumulative amount that you can deviate from your standard pricing formulas over the course of the year. The use of those discounts then becomes a part of your sales strategy. Be aware that this is an advanced technique and you need complete control of your costs, your projected sales, and pricing in order to be effective.
>
> **HIGHLIGHT 14**

Customer service is also sales

Kyle paused, "You buy and I'll tell you about customer service." An offer Ron couldn't refuse and he pick up the check from the table. Why did it seem that Kyle was waiting for Ron to pick up the check?

"Customer service is the handling of customers after the sale. If the only time you contact existing customers after the sale is when you are trying to collect money you are losing a tremendous opportunity. The best source of new business is in dealing with people who have used your service and have liked it. Systems of follow up are critical. How often are your customers contacted? How do you follow up the sale? What information do you gather? How do you use it? There is a treasure trove of information that your customers can give you regarding your own company—often times things that your employees will not tell you. Basic follow up on a regular basis can provide this information as well as referrals. Whenever collections are an issue there is never a system of effective follow-up from customer service."

Bidding, Estimating and Pricing

"Remember that in your business, estimating is a sales function." Ron was really getting his money's worth despite the fact that he felt the Rueben was overpriced. "Sales and Marketing brings to estimating a pre-determined amount of appropriate bid opportunities.[39] The responsibility of estimating is to accurately determine what the companies direct cost will be of each potential project (take-off). It is not the job of an estimator to determine the Price. Pricing is done according to the Sales Plan and incorporates the break even of the company and other company objectives. The estimator is held accountable for the accuracy of the bid—which creates the budget for the field. The job budget is what the field must focus upon—not the price. All incentives have to be based upon the budget."

"The market or your competitors cannot control pricing. Pricing must incorporate your real costs and pricing strategies based upon break even and company objectives. Pricing is an entirely separate function from the take off which is easily delegated."

Kyle seemed to have reached a stopping point. "What do you plan to do next?" she asked. "I think that I should approach the sales function just like any other function of the business. I need to identify the steps in lead generation, lead qualification, closing and customer service. I need to identify the results that are required of each function and develop positions to hire people for to fulfill those functions. I also need to make sure that the cost of the sales system is incorporated into the budget. Then I need to develop the KPI's and implement a staffing plan for the positions." Kyle was taken aback. "Do you know Tom?" she asked. "How do you know Tom?" "You answered my question. How is Judy?" "Fine. So how do you know Tom?" "We had the same teacher. Keep listening to him. Gotta go. Say "hi" to Judy for me." Kyle was checking her watch and moving towards the door before Ron could ask any more.

Ron spent the afternoon going over what Kyle had said. Building a sales structure intrigued him. When he got home Judy had left a note and gone out to a Tupperware party. "Where does all that Tupperware go anyway? Is there a Tupperware heaven? No luck tonight--might as well check my email." He had two from Tom.

The first was from an article. *"With few exceptions, the problem is not the sales force. Like most people... (the sales people) are extremely adept at selling things they believe in. More often the company has failed to create or identify the distinction that makes a selling message powerful, and that makes the salespeople true believers.....The key to any effective presentation is having a clear point of view. If you have one you believe in, you are almost certain to be effective in presenting it.....if your firm has not created or clearly identified its distinction, and the benefits of that distinction, to the people who use the service, most people will not present your case effectively for one simple reason: You haven't developed that case."*[40]

"By the way, sales Reps require the same management as inside sales people. As was stated earlier, the owner spends half of his time hitting numbers, and half of his time selling—of that half of the selling is external (customers) and half is internal—his own people. You must sell your sales force before they can sell you. All sales forces have to be managed. Sales people must be accountable. Commissions alone do not accomplish this end. Daily schedules and results must be monitored."

Sales is just a numbers formula:

(Number of contacts) x (the quality of the contacts) x (the quality of the presentation) x (the quality of the product) = number of sales.

How many leads must be generated? How should they be qualified? How should we present our product? How good is our product? If you are lacking in some areas you must do two things—in the short-term drive up higher numbers in the other areas to compensate for the weakness and in the long-term correct the weakness. Systems must be in place to monitor each of the variables so that weaknesses can be identified and acted upon. You cannot improve anything until you can measure it.

Tom

Ron turned to the cat, "I swear these guys have my phone tapped—he sounds just like Kyle!" The second email opened a new topic.

"By now you have read the sales book I left with you. I like the book but it only deals with one part of sales. You as the owner of a small business will always have some customers who need to deal with the owner. Therefore it is impossible to totally eliminate yourself from outside sales—and you shouldn't. You are good at it. But don't forget that external sales are only half of your sales function. The other half of the owner's sales function is **internal selling**. Few owners really understand this but if you think about it, it makes perfect sense. Internal selling is you selling your organization on the organizational structure that you have developed. <u>This is the most important function of company meetings!</u> Owners think that company meetings are for discussing clients or whatever other problems they have. These people are missing the point. That can be done individually or in a memo. The purpose of the company meeting is to provide you with a sales opportunity— an opportunity to continue to sell your organizational structure to your employees so that they will buy in to that structure and *therefore enforce the cost controls that produce the minimum mandatory percentage of profit that you need."*

Tom

"Might as well read the section on pricing labor—where does Tom get these books anyway? They are more binders than books and I never see them in libraries."

Ron found it under a Diet Pepsi can on the floor next to his desk. "To compute your labor rate use the following formula: (labor rate + burden)/gross profit. If the market cannot bear this rate, then you must also mark up materials in order to achieve your desired net profit." "Do I really want to go here tonight?" Ron took a bottle of Cabernet off the counter and put in the refrigerator. "Let's try this section on the cost of growth." "You have to evaluate your sales plan in the context of your company's ability to finance that growth. Sales growth causes a temporary <u>decrease</u> in cash. You have to pay the direct costs of your work before you get paid and therefore you turn cash into receivables. To compute the amount of cash that you will be required to finance your projected growth use the following formula: (Sales Growth x Direct Costs % divided by 365 times your collection rate) + additional overhead required to process the additional work. This gives you your cash or financing requirement." "Time to open the wine." The collection rate is found by dividing your average account receivables by your current annual sales and multiplying it by 365. Add to that amount any delay you have in posting the sales to your books.

"Honey—you're home! I fell asleep. Have some wine..." Ron had obviously had more than enough wine on his own. Judy was late and eyed the empty bottle on the table next to Ron.

The next morning came earlier for Judy than it did for Ron. He hadn't slept well on the couch. The daylight on his messy desk was calling him. Instead he sat on the couch with the television off and spent some time trying to think about the sales department at Acme but the beam of light through the window kept distracting him. Ron had not been involved in sales so now he was piecing together the parts that he knew. The company had a lot of low-paid people who spent their time calling potential customers. They turned their leads over to the more experienced inside sales people who qualified them and set appointments for their six sales "executives." These were people who knew what they were doing. Ron often interacted with them when they were putting together bids. Mr. O'Donoghue also got involved anytime the potential job was over $10,000.

The more he thought about it, the more he could identify the basic principles that had been laid out for him. On his computer he spent the next few hours outlining a sales system for his new company. He spent considerable time developing the performance variables that he wanted to track, how they would be tracked and how he would monitor them.

LABOR PRICING

(labor cost + burden)/desired Gross Profit

COST OF GROWTH

(Desired annual growth in $ x (1-Gross Profit) divided by 365 x collection rate) plus additional overhead required

COLLECTION RATE

Average Acct Receivables divided by Annual Sales x 365
Adjust by adding to this result any delay in posting sales

USP

A clear, concise statement of why a customer should buy from you instead your competitor.

HIGHLIGHT 15

Ron knew enough to be ready when Judy arrived home from work. He cleaned up the kitchen and then spent an hour and a half filing papers and cleaning up his desk area. Not relying on the brownie points from finally cleaning his desk, he also went to the store and had dinner ready when Judy walked in.

Judy recognized the effort when she walked through the door but decided to be mad a little longer. Finally after dinner and after Ron had cleaned up she gave in and picked up the legal pad. "So where are we now?"

Ron took the opening. "I have addressed sales just like any other part of the company. I laid out the tasks required for marketing, lead generation, lead qualification, closing, customer service, sales management and pricing and assigned them each to a position. From there I developed position guides. I want my customers to bond with the company instead of with a sales person." Judy was writing and Ron paused. When she looked up he continued.

"I also identified how I could use my meeting system to accomplish internal selling. I need to be constantly selling my employees on my system."

"What about pricing?" Judy asked. "Pricing formulas have to cover all costs—the direct cost of producing the product, the contribution to profit and the contribution to overhead. When I am above my break even I can reduce my price by discounting the amount of the fixed overhead which was paid through the previous sales. There is a formula for it that will really help." Judy finished writing, put down her pen and tore off the sheets. Handing them to Ron, Ron took the opportunity to give her a hug. She let him hug her for a while and then went to her purse. "I picked up a movie for tonight." Ron didn't need to see the title but knew he couldn't complain about her selection. The two hours were his penance.

Chapter Five – It's Not What You Make It's What You Keep[41]

After Ron has made money he must keep it.

Chapter Outline

1. **Legal entities**
2. **Tax Avoidance**
3. **Risk Management**
4. **Succession--value**

"There are five ways you can conduct business." William, Ron's lawyer, had agreed to see Ron again. The view was still stunning but Ron had a new confidence and sense of direction that was lacking in their first meeting. "You can operate as a sole proprietor, a partner, a limited partnership, a corporation or a limited liability corporation (LLC). The differences in these structures fall into two categories" William explained.

Liability. "The state statutes control one's exposure to liability. Sole Proprietors, partners and general partners in limited partnerships have unlimited personal liability. The company is sued and they can lose their personal assets. The purpose of incorporation is to limit your personal liability to the assets of the corporation. This is accomplished if you work with your attorney and aggressively respect the "corporate veil." In other words, you must treat the corporation as a separate entity and keep proper books and records. The corporation structure does not protect you if you are sued personally. Someone who successfully sues you personally for your personal actions can attach your assets and included in those assets are the shares of stock that you own in the corporation. About fifteen years ago the states started adopting a second kind of corporation called limited liability corporations (LLC). These are corporations with the same personal liability protections however they have one significant difference—if Ron of shares in an LLC is sued, the creditor can attach his property but cannot attach his shares in an LLC. This protects the company from "backdoor liability." It is virtual malpractice for a small business to operate as anything other than an LLC."

Taxation. "Taxation is a separate issue from liability. Taxation is handled by the federal government pursuant to the Internal Revenue Code (IRC). Under the IRC, if you operate as a sole proprietor, partner or general partner, the income or losses of the enterprise are your personal income. If you are a corporation (notice that an LLC is a corporation) then you can elect to file under either sub-chapter S or sub-chapter C of the IRC.[42] If you elect to file under sub-chapter S, then just like a sole proprietor the profit or losses are passed directly to you as your personal income. If you elect to file under sub-chapter C, then the corporation itself files its own tax return. There are advantages and disadvantages to both. Sub-chapter S is very beneficial when the company is losing money. The losses are passed directly to you and can offset other personal income. The disadvantages include the necessity to have a calendar year-end, the inability to take some deductions that sub-chapter C allows, and the problem with "phantom income." If the company shows a profit, then that is your income whether or not the company disburses cash. You can end up paying income tax at the highest tax scale on money that you don't even receive. Lazy accountants love to scare people from sub-chapter C with the argument that after the corporation pays its tax if you distribute dividends that money will be taxed again as personal income—double taxation. One must ask, "Who would be so stupid as to do that?" The fact is, the first $50,000 of income in a C corporation is taxed at 15% and most people don't take out all of the profit -from their business anyway. Right off the top one can save the difference between 33% and 15% tax on $50,000 of income through the use of a sub-chapter C election."[43]

"The fact is that there is no right structure for every business. If you think that you are paying too much in tax then you probably are. What is important is that you have an aggressive tax plan in place and constantly review it."

"If a person thinks that they are paying too much in taxes then they probably are. There are some companies that pay little tax and some that pay a lot. The common characteristic of those companies that pay little in tax is an aggressive tax avoidance *plan*. Those companies might have two entities—one a c-corporation and one an s-corporation so they can take advantage of all of the possible deductions. The s-corporation might not have a calendar year-end so that income can be timed and deferred. The company might choose to have one of the companies with only the key people as employees so that the benefit plan in that company can be enhanced. The c-corporation will show some income so that it is taxed at a rate much below the individual's tax rate but not so much income that they get involved in double-taxation. In a nutshell, they are actively trying to minimize their taxes instead of waiting to see what is due."

"You know what the definition of insanity is don't you Ron?" Ron didn't have time to answer. "Doing the same thing over and over again and expecting a different result!" William was very impressed with his line. "So many people just do the same thing over and over and expect that their tax problems will take care of themselves." "Those are the same people who do the same thing in their operations" Ron added.

William continued as if Ron hadn't responded. "Tax law is black, white and gray. Ron should venture into the gray. The gray is legal and legitimate; however it is more aggressive than the approach of most owners. *If you are never pushing into the gray, you are paying more than your fair share of tax and we can be sure that Uncle Sam will send you a thank-you letter. If you really want to help the government, pay your proper amount of taxes and make a donation.*"

"The potential estate taxes can be the most serious risk that a company faces. The IRS has a presumptive value on a company of 1.5 times sales.[44] That amount can then be taxed by up to 60% in an owner's estate causing the necessity to liquidate the business just to pay the taxes. Estate planning in the transition of a business is not a job for your general practice attorney. They don't know what they are doing and it will be too late when you find out. It is critical that expert advice be sought and second opinions obtained."

Financing

Ron thanked William for the review of his legal structure and hurried off to meet with a banker that Grace had recommended. He wanted to get there before lunchtime so he wouldn't have to buy him lunch.

"The issue of inadequate financing is actually a number of issues rolled into two questions: How much debt do they need? And why don't they already have it? In start-up situations inadequate capitalization is very common. The people started with inadequate capital and now want to maintain their equity position and substitute equity with debt. This is an entire issue in itself and requires more analysis than can be provided here. Suffice to say that if they need equity or a round of major funding, you first must have a valuation completed and then retain a competent mergers and acquisition firm. This is expensive and is not to be undertaken lightly—particularly since there can be no guarantees of its success." The banker, Moira, had been much more personable than Ron imagined bankers to be. Ron actually caught himself wishing he could take Moira to lunch. The thought was interrupted when Moira had to take a call from her husband. He wondered how Judy looked when he called.

"More commonly the company is just short of cash." Moira had hung up the phone and picked up where she had left off. The two most common causes of a cash shortage are uncontrolled growth and lack of profit. **These issues must be addressed because additional financing will not change them."**

"Often times the company doesn't have effective "sales tools" to use in obtaining financing. I see people come in here all of the time with a package that proves to me that I should not be lending them money! Calling on us at the bank is like making a sales call. If you called on a client and used sales materials similar to your tax accounting your conversation would go something like this, "this explains our product and as you can see it doesn't work very well. I want you to buy it and pay top dollar anyway." As absurd as this sounds one of the most common reasons why companies cannot get adequate financing is the quality of their "sales tools."

Ron was very pleased with his meetings with William and Moira. He felt that he had a handle on his business. He was a little disappointed when arrived home and there was not an email waiting for him. He made a lunch—he didn't need to tell Judy about his "lunch" at 4:00—from the leftovers in the refrigerator and sent out a question for Tom. He could see now that an exit strategy was important but he had never been involved in the sale of a business. He was not surprised when a response came back before he made minutes.

Inability to sell the business

A people dependent business cannot be sold. A symptom of a People Dependent business arises in hiring. Some owners hire employees to do tasks that they do not do well themselves. They try to hire a "hot-shot." They want someone with "experience." Basically they want to hire someone who can tell them how to run that aspect of their business. This is the mentality of someone who will be forever trapped in a People Dependent business. Their new hire will be expensive, hard to replace, will hold them hostage and limit the company's achievement to their level of competency.

Before you can hire anyone, you have to have a job. The job comes first, the person comes second. The job must be defined. The expected results must be defined. You have done this and done it well. It is your system—it is your risk—and you could not have abdicated that responsibility. As you have discovered, defining the positions is a large part of your job. You will own a business not a job. You will run it, it won't run you. You will be able to sell it if you choose.

Often the owner is holding the business hostage. There can be no real value to the business until it can run without him."

Tom

Judy walked in the door carrying a bottle of Pinot Grigio and wearing a big grin. "Got a raise today—want to celebrate?" So much for work tonight.

Ron placed the legal pad on Judy's placemat. She sighed as she came to the table. "This week was great. I know that whatever I make I have to keep and I learned about tax avoidance, risk management and succession planning—ready for notes?" Judy hesitated. She had a grin that would make a Cheshire cat proud. "Why don't you pull out the notes from our last four sessions?" Ron was confused, but did as he was told. He had taken each set of notes and put them in a manila envelope on his desk. "I haven't really reviewed them yet" he stammered. "Well read them then." He pulled them out. After a confused moment he started to laugh. "Four score and seven years ago…" Each of the sets of notes were copies of the Gettysburg Address. "You didn't really think I had any idea of what you were talking about did you?" Ron just smiled.

Chapter Six – Are We Having Fun Yet?

Ron must be having fun—are we having fun yet?

Chapter Outline

   1. Own a business; not a job

Ron had one more stop to make. He wanted to visit Dusty, his old classmate who owned his own business. He had called Dusty numerous times but had been unable to get him to the phone. He called his wife and Christina just mused on about the hours that Dusty works and how miserable they both are. Dusty was working long hours, there were constant employee problems and they were losing money instead of making it. Ron drove by and spent an hour in the business. Dusty was only able to speak to with him for a few minutes. He had to work the counter, he had to answer the phone, he had to deal with a creditor—he never had a minute to himself. Ron finally gave up, promised Dusty that he'd stop by again and Dusty apologized promising that he would have more time for him next time.

Stuck in traffic it took Ron over an hour to get home—some RV had misjudged the height of an overpass. The drive did give him a lot of time to think. Christina's concerns had also been Judy's concerns and as depressing as Dusty's situation was, Ron recognized the problem. He also vowed never to drive an RV.

"Dusty is working excessive hours because he is doing other people's jobs. He has no system other than to work as hard as he can and his delegation techniques must be improved. Dusty must learn to understand how to keep "the monkey" on the back of others so that he doesn't turn into a "zookeeper." In fact Ron is spending more time doing other people's jobs than he is doing his own. His job is to run the company and in fact the company is running him." Ron and Judy were sitting in the living room with their bottle of wine. Judy just listened as Ron talked on. "**Working in the business means doing the tasks that should be done by and employee. Working on the business means doing the tasks that should be done by Dusty. Dusty doesn't own a business he owns a job—and he is working for an idiot.**"

Ron was on a roll now. "An owner starts his own business in order to achieve his goal of being his own boss. He discovers that he may not have a direct supervisor anymore but his income is still dependent upon him performing the same tasks that he performed in his employment and in addition to that he is swamped in "paperwork" and employee problems. He may (or more likely may not) have a greater income, but his hours and responsibilities are so greatly increased that all he has is a bigger job than the one he left. If he had put in this many hours and this much effort for his former employer he would probably be ahead of where he is now. All that he tried to achieve was self-employment and he has achieved that."

"There is a significant difference between owning a business and owning a job. **Having a business means that he makes his money off the efforts of others, rather than off the efforts of his own. You should make money off of every employee; therefore any business with employees should make money.**"

Owning a job

"Some people are content with a job. As long as they are content with the hours, inability to get away, and their current compensation then they need not be changed. When a person has a job they end up with excessive work hours. They are doing the job of one or more employees and trying to do their own job (run the company). They cannot get away because systems and controls have never been established that allow them to delegate the functions of operations to others. They have no way to really know that the functions are being properly done without being there. Their compensation is limited to the number of hours that they are willing (or able) to work. They have no hope of opening a second location because the operations depend upon the personal attention of Ron and he can only be in one place. They can never sell their business because <u>they are the business.</u> If they left, there would be no business. Eventually the assets are sold but they years of sweat equity go uncompensated. They are good at some of the tasks and not as good at others. As their business grows they are required to do more and more tasks that they are not good at. Eventually they get overwhelmed, fail to grow and die."

Owning a business

Judy broke in, "Let's have something to eat with the next bottle." "Good idea honey" and the conversation moved to the kitchen but didn't slow. "A business owner owns a few hard assets and his systems. Why does a 1000 square foot building sell for hundreds of thousands of dollars if it is a McDonalds? Because it has ironclad systems that produce a pre-determined return based upon location. McDonalds is completely SYSTEMS DEPENDENT. Most small businesses are PEOPLE DEPENDENT. McDonald's systems allow for the least qualified person in each position and they are so strong that the people are irrelevant to the success of the business. Most small businesses purposely become dependent upon the most qualified person in each position and become held hostage by their employees. Since the value of most small business pales in comparison to the value of McDonalds, we can assume that a SYSTEMS DEPENDENT business is better than a PEOPLE DEPENDENT business. **This can only be achieved through a conscious effort on the part of Ron to do his job rather than other people's jobs."**

"In order to own a business you must <u>try</u> to own a business. That means that significant time and resources must be spent working on the business rather than working in the business."

Dusty is in the eye of the hurricane. He is trying to get from where he is to where he wants to be. In his way are all of the issues that I have been looking at. Taken separately he can probably address each one; however none of the issues can be taken separately." "What you are saying is that crisis management is caused by Dusty focusing upon these issues a few at a time rather than employing a comprehensive attack in a logical, professional manner." Judy was impressed with the wisdom of Chardonnay. So was Ron and a peck on the cheek reward precluded his further explanation. "As the company currently operates, one problem comes to the forefront and Dusty deals with it--then the next problem and the next problem. Dusty deals with these problems in the order of their short-term pain. <u>This is a perpetual cycle of fixing what has broken and never building a machine that will achieve the higher result.</u>"

"The only logical and effective action is to develop a comprehensive plan of attack on all of the existing and projected problems and launch a coordinated attack." Ron now understands the appropriate systems, procedures and controls needed to break this cycle and achieve success.

The doorbell rang. Judy started to pick things up and throw away a wine bottle or two as Ron headed to the door. "Is this a bad time?" Ron was stunned. There stood Tom, Grace and his father. "Come on in" Ron stammered as he picked up the coat he had left by the door. "How do you guys know Dad?" was all he could think to say. "Your Dad was our teacher" Tom said. Grace just nodded. "He knew that you wouldn't listen to him, so we did him a favor."

"From what they say, son you are ready."

Epilog

If there is one thing to take from this story it is that what you own when you own a small business is not the people, the equipment, or anything tangible. What you own is a system. A system for producing cash from the market demand for your good or service. How well you document and how much you invest in the development of that system of converting market demand into cash will have a direct relationship to your success. You must develop a systems dependent business, not a people dependent business. You still need good people, but just as much or more you need a good system.

In 2003, a client relayed to me the obvious—that software should be developed to implement the concepts of "Minding My Own Business." Although it took nearly a year, the time was worth it. Your business now can truly have an "operating system."

While completing your system, remember that there is only one reason for your business to exist—to make your life better. Identify what is making your life better and expand upon it; identify what is making your life worse and get rid of it. Build your system to produce a result that will make your life better.

I hope you enjoyed your travels with Ron.

Appendix I

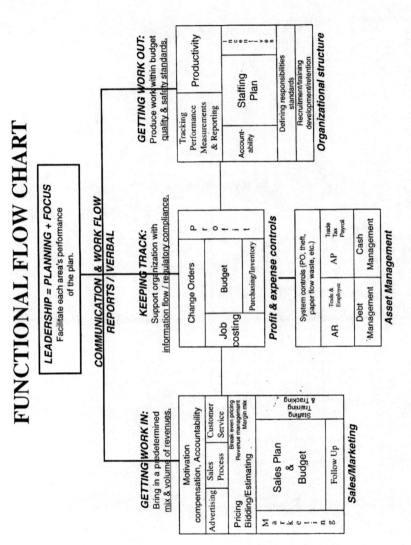

113

Appendix II - Worksheets

When an early draft of this work was reviewed by a client in Minneapolis it was suggested that software be developed to follow the text. What resulted is The Fremont Business Operating System™. Any business owner can take this software and make a significant change in their company. When the owner uses a Fremont mentor to assist, on-going change becomes a reality.

> **The software can be purchased on our web site**
> **WWW.THE-FREMONT-GROUP.COM**

The following Appendix pages are drawn from the software. The software is written in Microsoft Word and Excel.[45] You will need basic skills in these programs, however you do not need any knowledge other than how to write in Word and how to fill in (no formulas) in Excel. On the Excel files look for the red triangles. When you place your curser on a red triangle you receive instructions and hints--how to fill out the forms, how to print the forms, and helpful information. Be sure to read them all. Also be alert for red warnings and instructions popping up—these are to make sure that you are not only using the program properly but that you are also developing a plan without internal contradictions.

Open first the security warning file and the welcome file. These are both in Word. They document the contents of the program and give you some basic background information. Then print the first pages of the Excel workbook "Worksheets." These give you a flow chart for tasks.

The first real task is the Goal Sheet. Everyone has made resolutions for the New Year—and everyone has broken them. They are broken from a lack of effective follow up. The Fremont Business Operating System™ prevents this from happening. I was once told (by Tom?) that, "a goal without a plan is only a wish." By using FBOS you will attach a plan to your goals. The initial pages ask the business owner to write out specific goals. What do you want revenues to be in one year? In three years? What do you want the business to look like? How much cash do you want to retain? Follow the program answering each question recording your answer in the yellow areas only.

On a spreadsheet, the owner first identifies their goals. The process is directed through a series of questions. Next to each goal you must identify the tasks that are required to accomplish your goal. These are the actions that must be taken. Responsibility for each action is then assigned to a person within the company. Now you have someone accountable for achieving the defined tasks. Next is follow-up.

The follow-up is accomplished through a meeting schedule. There are quarterly meetings, monthly meetings and weekly meetings (in addition to your daily huddles.) These meetings do not have to be long and it is often best to schedule them over a normally non-productive time—lunch or breakfast. The dates and times of the meetings are generated through your input on the sheets. The meeting agendas are also produced in the sheets that follow your goals and they carry over to them for the agenda the requirement of the responsible person to report progress at the appropriate times for each of your assigned tasks. Now you have goals instead of wishes.

Also included on this spreadsheet are forms for the daily huddle sign in, for each "committee" to keep their action points from their meeting, and for the owner to complete his or her own review of progress on a weekly, monthly and quarterly basis.

The owner should purchase a three-ring binder for each year. Twelve dividers for the months are nice but not required. Each monthly Profit & Loss Statement and Balance Sheet should be inserted into the Company Log, and behind each should be inserted the pages from the meetings. The requirement that these be turned in to you is a focus technique. The employees understand that they have to turn in to the owner a summery of what they have done for each period on each topic. You are now focusing their actions upon the accomplishment of your goals—duh!

Concurrent with the development of the goals should be the development of the financial data—some of which might be required for your goals or might cause you to alter some of your goals. The data from the summary financial statements should be entered on in the workbook "Worksheets." Spending some time in this workbook will generate all sorts of useful information. Pay particular attention to the budget page.

If you are ever confused about what some of the information or terms are, go back to the index of "Minding My Own Business."

The worksheets walk the owner through the budget development process and create profit and expense controls. They identify your annual loss, quickly review your AR and liquidity positions, and develops pricing schemes and sales strategies for use of discounts from your pricing scheme (break even pricing). The program also checks to see that your budget is in line, and that your financial "game plan" is designed to "win the game." From your data, KPI's are identified. You will assign people to be held accountable for their achievement and integrate reporting of that progress into your meeting system.

Also developed in this process is the Cash Flow Forecasting System. When properly implemented, this system is your most powerful cash management tool.

In the worksheets marked "sample" fictitious data has been entered. It gives you a feel for how your final product might look.

The third leg of the stool is the Quantitative Analysis of Functionality. This worksheet completely compiles your organizational structure. Proper use of this worksheet will eliminate gaps and duplication in your structure, will increase productivity, will provide methods of accountability and ultimately creates an incentive plan. On the first page enter each position and the chain of command. Also on that page is the information flow—enter how information is to flow in your system. Then each functional area of the business is given a worksheet. Every task that is required in each department of the company is entered.[46] Each task is identified, the result required is established and then they are recorded on the sheet. The task is assigned to the desired position in the company.

The Sales sheet is divided into the sales functions—lead generation, lead qualification, closing, customer service and management. In conjunction with the Sales sheet, you should also develop your USP. A Word file has been established for this task. Each task requires a position—the position must be listed on the Communications Chart (first sheet of the workbook.)

The second sheet is the Operations section. Departments are identified by the user. These are the tasks that are required to produce your work. The final department is management. Typically these are GM tasks. The final sheet is the Administrative section. Administration "keeps track and manages the company" rather than the sales function which "brings the work in to the company" or the operations function which "gets the work out the door."

The completion of these sheets are not small tasks. You will think that you are finished and then you will add tasks to them. Remember that you do not "fix" a business—this is a journey and not a destination. Regular review and up-date of "your system" is mandatory but you have to start somewhere. When you think that you are close to having entered in all of the tasks you now create the Position Guides.

Creation of the Position Guides requires some Excel manipulation. On the page "Position Guides" each of the positions that you have listed in the Communications Chart (first sheet) have been carried over. Go to the first position and find the job title. Then go back to the three sheets (Sales, Operations and Administration) and for each department click on the down arrow in the box and choose this job title. It will filter the column below it and only display the tasks that you have assigned to that position. Shade those tasks, hold down the "control" key while you hit the "c" key. This is prepare these items to be copies and it will create a box around the shaded area that seems to be moving. Immediately go back to the "Position Guides" page and on the proper line put he curser and hit "enter." This should then copy the entries onto the page. Then return to the sheet where you used the filter and use it again this time choosing the selection "all." This returns the page to its' original view. Then repeat the process for each department of each of the three sheets.[47]

Your Position Guides are now developed. Fill in the remainder of the information creating a review process for the employee. It might be appropriate to wait to do the Incentive section until your first revision for the same reason that parents don't start talking to their kids about the trip to Disneyworld until they are sure that they can get off work and afford it!

The last section is the compilation of those position guides into the development of the Operations Manual. Following each position guide, take each task and write out how it should be done. This information—and a lot of the data required to complete the tasks entered on the position guides can be obtained through the input of your employees. Let them document what they are doing, you modify it, and then compile it.

The Fremont Business Operating System™ creates a logical, and complete system allowing the business owner to obtain control of their business. For more information about The Fremont Business Operating System™, to purchase the software or to contract for the assistance of a mentor to implement the system or to find up-dated versions of the software visit the Fremont Group's web site at www.the-fremont-group.com.

Some people will be able to fully implement FBOS without assistance. All people will benefit from the experience of trying even portions of the software, however for the vast majority of business owners, there are some portions that they can complete and some portions that will require help. The Fremont Group provides mentors to assist in the development of the system—however their value to the business owner then continues as the system requires continuous implementation. Having a mentor (Tom again?) who helped develop your system, understands you and your system, is invaluable in the on-going journey towards your goals. We hope to hear from you!

© 2004 Dirk T. Dieters; THE FREMONT GROUP

The Fremont Group

The Fremont Group is a firm of experienced former business owners who work locally to serve small businesses on a long-term basis. Our clients believe that there is nothing like calling your own shots. When you are free to do that, the business will usually move along the way you want it to, and you wind up being able to do anything you want with it. We provide the systems, procedures and controls that you need to be successful in our increasingly competitive environment. When you have everything running like clockwork, you don't have people knocking on your door and turning your world upside down. You are able to keep things on track and maintain control over what's really important. We provide hands-on management mentoring—you provide the technical knowledge.

The Fremont Group

Administrative Center & Denver Office

(303) 338 9300

WWW.THE-FREMONT-GROUP.COM

End Notes

[1] <u>The E-Myth,</u> Michael E. Gerber, Harper Collins, 1989.

[2] In this entire work, the masculine pronoun is used for convenience only.

[3] The Fremont Group has developed software that accompanies the text of "Minding My Own Business." The Fremont Group Business Operating System™ incorporates all of the calculations and principles of the book.

[4] Sometimes revenue will be referred to as "sales" or "income."

[5] Direct costs are "Cost of Goods Sold" or COGS.

[6] Tom's analysis ignores depreciation. Depreciation is a "non-cash" expense meaning that you do not have to write a check for the expense. Non-cash expenses reduce your profit (and taxes) without compromising your cash flow. You do have to write a check for new asset purchases and these are not expenses. New assets are purchased with "after-tax" dollars. You budget for new asset purchases in your profit plan (how you plan to use your profit.) In that profit plan you also budget for cash retention. In well run businesses your cash retention should exceed your scheduled depreciation. Otherwise you will have to finance new purchases to replace the worn out equipment.

[7] This subject is more completely addressed in the Managerial Accounting section under Profit Treated as a Residual.

[8] See also, <u>Who Moved My Cheese.</u>

[9] <u>Moments of Truth</u>, Jan Carlzon, HarperPerennial 1989

[10] ibid

[11] <u>The Everett Business Journal</u>, September 2000.

[12] "Nobody puts a proposal for a new comprehensive strategy on your desk and asks you to make a decision about it. You have to put it there yourself. And once you use your view of the big picture to formulate a strategy, you have to call on a wide range of skills to achieve a series of objectives. You must devise a business strategy tailored to your goal. You need to communicate the goal and strategy to…all the employees. You have to give greater responsibility to people at the front line and then create a secure atmosphere where they will dare to use their new authority. You must build an organization that can work to achieve the goal and establish measures that guarantee you are moving in the right direction. In short, you have to create the prerequisites for making the vision a reality." <u>Moments of Truth</u>, Jan Carlzon, HarperPerennial 1989.

[13] <u>Moments of Truth</u>, Jan Carlzon, HarperPerennial 1989

[14] It is important to keep your information needs in the proper perspective. Ron must first create a plan—a vision—and identify what it is that they are trying to achieve. An important part of that plan is the financial plan as discussed herein. Once established, the company's organizational structure becomes the delivery system of those results. Each job requires a defined result and that result is determined by your plan. Organizational Structure is examined in Part II. Finally the information systems monitor those results. Their purpose is to alert Ron as to whether or not he is performing his plan.

[15] The topic of accountability and incentives is covered extensively in the organizational structure section.

[16] Colonel Savage, upon observing the workers of the Union Pacific RR in 1868, "Verily, men earn their money like horses and spend it like asses."

[17] The proper way of computing your collection rate is to divide your average accounts receivable by your annual sales and then multiply by 365.

[18] The cost of not having the money includes the borrowing costs and lost opportunity costs in not being able to take discounts, etc. The income from having the money is your return on assets.

[19] As the monitor of the material costs is a percentage of revenues, all of these factors can be correct and the problem can fall in pricing. A Company cannot have control of material costs if you have a random system of pricing or if a company fails to have systems of up-dating pricing based upon the doctrine of true costs.

[20] KPI's must be developed in any equipment intensive business to measure equipment utilization.

[21] <u>Moments of Truth</u>, Jan Carlzon, HarperPerennial 1989

[22] The Fremont Group has developed software—Fremont Business Operating System—that assist owners in the steps required to establish an "operating system" for their business.

[23] Even a receptionist can have job standards—answer the phone before the third ring 95% of the time, answer the phone a specific way 100% of the time, etc.

[24] See the Problem Area: Budget

[25] This is the basic flaw in profit sharing. Individual employees cannot control the profit of the company—Ron does. The individual employee can only control the result that is delegated to them. Bonuses must be based upon their performance alone.

[26] Effective management is getting a group of people to do something that they would not ordinarily do and enjoy doing it. (Paraphrased Douglas McArthur)

[27] "Danger in the Comfort Zone" Judith Bardwick. HarperPress 1990.

[28] Competent management mentors and consultants can survey your employees to determine their relative fear vs entitlement mode and can assist you in developing corrective actions.

[29] 480 minutes in the workday; 45 wasted on breaks, potty time, slow starts, getting ready for lunch and end of the day leaving 435 minutes per day. 24/435 = 5.5% To compute the cost of this 5.5% to your business take your total annual wages and multiply it by .055 and you will then understand the importance of controlling it.

[30] First Things First, Stephen Covey, Simon & Schuster 1994. If you are to read one of Covey's books, 7 Habits of Highly Successful People, is the book to read. In First Things First, Covey covers some of the same ground but gets much more technical in his analysis.

[31] Ibid.

[32] Moments of Truth, Jan Carlzon, HarperPerennial 1989

[33] One of the first elements of team building in an organization is to clearly define how the team should function and then "sell" that attitude to each incoming employee. For example, "As an employee here we expect three things—that you at all times exhibit a positive attitude, that you at all times work as a team and that at all times you use our system. These are conditions of working here. If you decide that you cannot comply with these conditions, please do not submit your application for employment."

[34] Often confused is the difference between the "Employee Handbook" and an Operations Manual. The Employee Handbook is for meeting legal requirements (non-discrimination policies, etc.). The Operations Manual or the Policies and Procedures Guide is the codification of each job

procedure. How you want things done. This includes the job descriptions and results, incentives and accountability, and the mission statement of the company. Many people merge the two documents.

[35] As Ron redoes this documentation of his system each year, he is able to enroll the assistance of his employees by asking them to compile a list of all of the tasks that they perform in the course of their job. He uses this to redo the job descriptions and the incentive plan.

[36] Positioning, Al Ries and Jack Trout,

[37] Selling the Invisible, Harry Beckwith, Warner Books, Inc. 1997

[38] In the Budget section you will see that the break even sales plan requires sales equaling the amount required in the profit plan divided by the net profit.

[39] This is how you hold Sales and Marketing accountable. The company plan sets the standards as to what an appropriate bid opportunity is and how many opportunities per week/month/quarter or whatever they should generate. This of course is based upon the bid to award ratio.

[40] Selling the Invisible, Harry Beckwith, Warner Books, 1997.

[41] The reader is warned NOT TO RELY UPON THIS FOR LEGAL OR TAX ADVICE. Laws and tax codes constantly change. Understand the concepts and then discuss them with your tax and legal professional.

[42] Note that in many states an LLC is taxed as a general partnership.

[43] Tax laws change quickly but the principles generally remain the same. Check with your accountant for up-to-date information.

[44] This information is derived from an interview with a former IRS investigator. It is not consistent across the country or between offices and is subject to change.

[45] Microsoft Word and Excel are registered trademarks of the Microsoft Corporation.

[46] You will find this an on-going process. Following your first use you will continually add tasks to the lists.

[47] If this process has seemed incredibly confusing to you, employ the assistance of someone in your office with better Excel skills. Once shown how to do this, it is not difficult.

About The Author

Dirk Dieters has a BA from Michigan State University and his J.D. from Detroit College of Law. He has owned his own business and is the founder of The Fremont Group, a respected national management consulting firm. Mr. Dieters has worked with nearly 1000 small businesses. His observations are reflected in his writing.